MY BOOK OF ABSURD LET[TERS TO SCOT]TISH FOOTBALL CLUBS BY

STRUAN J. MARJORIBANKS

A SCRAPBOOK OF
FOOTBALLING MADNESS
COMPILED BY

FRASER SYME

eat the breed

IF YOU BUY
THIS BOOK AND
BRING IT TO MY
HOUSE I WILL GIVE YOU
A CUP OF TEA AND
A CUSTARD CREAM...

Best Wishes

a.k.a

'MY BOOK OF ABSURD LETTERS TO BRITISH
FOOTBALL CLUBS BY STRUAN J. MARJORIBANKS'

ISBN: 978-0-9929353-0-6

Cover design & layout by Craig Lamont.

Renfrewshire, Scotland

FOREWORD BY THE AUTHOR

There probably comes a time in most people's working lives when they develop such an unhealthy dislike for people that they start to wonder if it's actually them that is the doo-doo head. That's not what happened to me, but it must be just awful. During the afternoon of the 10th of October 2007 I should have been keeping up the pretence of understanding what I was doing in my financial services job, but instead I sent a bizarre (bordering on mentally ill) email to my friend Panos. Hi Panos (he's Greek). Without a second thought I signed the email 'Struan J. Marjoribanks,' and that is how Struan entered this world. Struan now lives in my head, and like most other people round these parts he sleeps in a bed. Under Struan's bed there is an old shoebox – a shoebox which once housed the trainers his father wore to badminton on Thursday nights. Stored in that shoebox are all things dear to Struan: his absurd letters to football clubs, his customised Panini sticker albums, his cartoon depictions of future television appearances, and, of course, some other stuff. It was while hoovering under Struan's bed one Sunday afternoon that I found the shoebox, and so intrigued was I by its well-thumbed contents that I scanned each and every one of them before putting them back just as I had found them. Had Struan's collection been any good then I would simply have sent the scans off to publishers claiming them as my own, but as they were really quite poor I just copied his ideas. *Et voilà* – my book! He will be furious.

Fraser Syme

THANKS

To my wife Catriona – you didn't write any of the book or come up with any ideas or anything, but you never complained about getting mail which didn't relate to us at all. Thanks for that. To my sons Cameron and Andrew – you genuinely make me the luckiest dad in the world, and I hope that someday you can show your friends your dad's work and feel proud to be his son. I'll write something else that you can do that with. To Craig Lamont (designer extraordinaire) – many thanks for making this happen and for showing such remarkable patience with me. I simply couldn't have done this without you. Actually, maybe I could have, but the book would be really rubbishy, and I couldn't very well meet myself for lunch to talk about Panini stickers and fonts, could I? To my parents, my sister Heather, and her family – thanks for being so interested and for feeding me so fantastically well, it really is appreciated even if I don't say anything or speak to you for quite long periods of time. To Jamie the coach (I said you'd get a mention and this is it) – thanks. To Big Gazz, Gumbo, Gusty and all the other boys from the Inverclyde Darts League – cheers boys, I miss you all! To Gus, Dolph, IC, Frasbo, Archie, Leg, Panos, Craig and any friends that I've missed – thanks boys, without all the nonsense over the years there would be no book.

To the football clubs (and companies) who responded to the letters – I simply cannot thank you enough. Without your responses there is nothing and it is to your eternal credit that you took the time to reply to Struan. To Panini – thanks for letting me use your wonderful work! Swapping your stickers in the playground is the only thing I remember enjoying at school between the ages of six and eleven (there was nothing at all after that).

I would also like to thank Adam Stansfield who kindly signed the portrait painted by Struan's son. Adam tragically passed away in August 2010 having been diagnosed with colorectal cancer. I was greatly saddened when I heard this, and if any readers would like to learn more about Adam's story or make a donation to the foundation set up in his memory then please visit:

www.adamstansfieldfoundation.com

Finally, if you've bought this book (providing it wasn't for 99p in one of those cheapo book shops) then I am extremely grateful. If you're reading this but haven't decided whether to buy or not, I have two small children who often go without due to the volume of stamps that I am required to buy. Your support really is greatly appreciated!

SOUTH OF ENGLAND

- 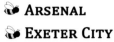 ARSENAL
- EXETER CITY
- PORTSMOUTH
- BRIGHTON & HOVE ALBION
- CHELSEA
- PETERBOROUGH UTD
- HAVANT & WATERLOOVILLE
- WEST HAM UTD

struan's south of england facts

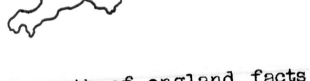 many people who live or work in central london do not own a watch due to the relative ease with which they can see big ben

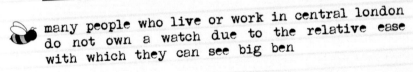 the snowmen built by street urchins in this area rarely consist of less than 5% dog's woop

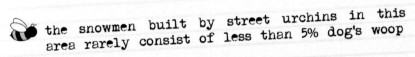 brighton is the hoarding capital of great britain, with hundreds of hoarders relocating there every year

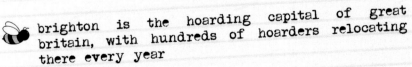 represents the land of milk and honey (mainly honey)

4th January 2010

Ms Penny Downs
Customer Service Manager
Arsenal Football Club
Highbury House
75 Drayton Park
London, N5 1BU

Dear Ms Downs,

It is not in my nature to write a letter of complaint, so I ask that you please bear with me.

I watched Arsenal's match against Aston Villa on television on December 27th with my son Daniel (8) and we enjoyed it greatly. However, at one point in the match the fans of your club sang a song which went along the lines of 'if you don't support Arsenal you are a loser.' I don't think that those were the exact words of the song, but that was the gist of it.

Daniel is not an Arsenal supporter as such (Hibernian daft he is) and he happens to be quite a sensitive lad. Sensing that he was under attack Daniel asked me what the Arsenal fans were singing as he couldn't quite make out the words. Thinking on my feet I pretended that they were singing something else entirely, but Daniel wouldn't let it go. Eventually I had to tell him that I thought they were singing that he was a loser (I am an Arsenal fan so it didn't relate to me).

Naturally Daniel was very upset and although I asked him not to take it personally he felt that as he was enjoying watching Arsenal's match (as he always does) that the fans shouldn't be so mean. I found it hard to disagree and consequently Daniel says that he will never watch an Arsenal match again.

I appreciate that this kind of issue may be outside of your remit, but I have a disappointed and hurt son and felt that I should bring this to your club's attention. I would be interested to know what your club's policy is on this kind of thing, and what as a club you would say to Daniel by way of an apology?

I hope that all made sense as like I said at the beginning I do not find complaining easy. I look forward to hearing your thoughts and hope that as a result I will be able to prove to Daniel that Arsenal is a great club after all.

Best Wishes,

Struan J. Marjoribanks

2

24th January 2010

The Premier League
Customer Services Department
30 Gloucester Place
London, W1U 8PL

Dear Sir/Madam,

On the 6th of January of this year I sent a letter of complaint to Arsenal Football Club, and it is with considerable regret that I inform you that I have yet to receive a response. I have been informed that Arsenal state on their website that all complaints will be responded to within seven days, and I therefore do not feel that I am being unreasonable in bringing my complaint to your attention some eighteen days later. I trust that you will agree on the reasonability of this.

I will cut what is quite a long story as short as possible. I was watching Arsenal's match against Aston Villa on 27/12/09 with my son Daniel (8). Unlike myself Daniel is not an Arsenal fan (Hibs daft) and he took great offence to a song being sung by the supporters of Arsenal Football Club.

I asked Arsenal Football Club to advise what their policy is on offensive chanting and what they would say as a club by way of an apology to Daniel. No response has been received from Arsenal, and with each day that passes Daniel's resentment towards myself (for being an Arsenal fan) and Arsenal Football Club multiplies exponentially.

The postman's daily visit sees Daniel rushing to the door hoping to find a letter from Arsenal Football Club which could make everything alright again. Instead Daniel is left heartbroken as credit card statements, junk mail pertaining to budget German supermarkets, and brochures for holiday cottages in Cumbria (we went there once!) flood through our letterbox instead.

My letter to Arsenal was addressed to their Customer Services Manager, Penny Downs, who I suspect you may be familiar with. If you could now take up my complaint with Arsenal Football Club I would be extremely grateful as it appears that they do not have the courtesy to respond to me directly.

Daniel and I eagerly await your response and we thank you in advance for fighting our corner.

Best Wishes,

Struan J. Marjoribanks   3

29 January 2010

Mr Struan J Marjoribanks

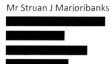

Dear Struan

I have been informed by the Premier League that you have not received my letter dated 8 January 2010. I am therefore enclosing the same together with the goodwill gesture that was sent on that day.

I have sent this special delivery to ensure that you receive this. Once again as per the letter, please feel free to contact me on 0207 704 4438.

Kind regards

Yours sincerely

Penny Downs
Customer Services Manager

4

Arsenal Charity 2009/2010
www.gosh.org Registered Charity No. 235825
2007 Great Ormond Street Hospital Children's Charity

SUPPORTER SERVICES
HIGHBURY HOUSE
75 DRAYTON PARK
LONDON N5 1BU

TELEPHONE: +44 (0)20 7619 5000
FAX: +44 (0)020 7704 4161
www.arsenal.com

8 January 2010

Mr Struan J Marjoribanks

Dear Struan

Thank you for taking the time and trouble to write in with your complaint. I have to admit that it as one of the more unusual complaints that we receive in to Arsenal Football Club.

The main gist of your complaint is that Arsenal fans were heard to sing a song along the lines of; "If you don't support the Arsenal, you're a loser". I have to confess that I did not hear this particular song, nor is it a regular song that is heard here at the Emirates. That notwithstanding, clearly Daniel heard the song and took the song to heart with him being a supporter of Hibernian as you state.

In common with all Premier League clubs, we do have a policy regarding offensive chants and we take a very firm stance on supporters that choose to ignore this policy.

However, in this instance, I personally feel that whilst the song was negative to other supporters, it was not offensive in terms of race, sexual orientation or an incitement to violence. I think that in common with fans up and down we all feel that our own club is the best and everyone else's is at best not as good as our own, or at worst rubbish. I think in this instance the Arsenal supporters were voicing their pride in the Club by being negative towards other supporters.

Indeed as a Hibernian supporter, your son will at some time hear some far worse songs from the local rivals – Hearts. A quick review on their fans websites reveal some quite pointed references to Hibs and their fans.

I think my message to your son would be to take pride in his own team, and realise that songs sung in football grounds are not meant to be taken too seriously and also to have a joke with his Dad and ask "Who's the loser" when inevitably Arsenal lose a match in the future.

By way of a goodwill gesture, whilst I realise he doesn't support Arsenal, we have included some squad cards within the letter (marked for his attention) and an "Inside Arsenal" that he might find interesting to read.

5

Great
Ormond
Street
Hospital
Charity
Arsenal Charity 2009/2010
www.gosh.org Registered Charity No. 235825
2007 Great Ormond Street Hospital Children's Charity

The Arsenal Football Club Plc - Company Registration Number 109244 England

If you have any questions or queries, or would like to speak to me regarding any of the content of this reply, then please feel free to contact me on 0207 704 4438.

Kind regards

Yours sincerely

PD.

Penny Downs
Customer Services Manager

Ms Penny Downs
Customer Service Manager
Arsenal Football Club
Highbury House
75 Drayton Park
London, N5 1BU

Dear Ms Downs,

I can't remember ever receiving a Special Delivery package before so I am extremely grateful to you for the lovely surprise which Daniel and I received on Saturday morning.

Where your original letter dated 8th of January went is a complete mystery and will unfortunately remain that way – a little bit like the Loch Ness Monster, or the moon being made of cheese. But seriously, it was ever so kind of you to re-send your letter and the package of goodies for Daniel.

I would like to make it clear that I had not intended to step on your tootsies by contacting the Premier League and I hope that my actions caused you no upset.

I was delighted to read that as a club you do not tolerate offensive chanting, and perhaps the 'loser chant' (as we now call it) has simply slipped through the net. I am also very pleased to report that your goodwill gesture towards Daniel has turned him round a little.

The *Inside Arsenal* guide was devoured by Daniel (and myself!) and what a fascinating little pamphlet it is. The squad cards were also gratefully received and although Daniel initially branded the players featured as 'Big Money Sick Notes' he soon came round to your way of thinking.

Spot on about those Hearts fans by the way. Those *Hearties* can be a bad lot and they chant some stuff that would make your hair curl.

Finally, Arsenal did go and lose 1-3 to Manchester United at the Emirates Stadium yesterday didn't they?! So you can guess who has been getting it tight ever since.....

Thanks again for your explanation of the situation, your generosity, and for helping my son realise that Arsenal Football Club ain't so bad after all. Come on you Gunners!!

Best Wishes,

Struan J. Marjoribanks

9

Mr Struan J Marjoribanks

Dear Mr Marjoribanks,

Thank you for your recent letter with regard to your letter of complaint addressed to Penny Downs at Arsenal Football Club.

We have spoken to Arsenal about your complaint and they have sent us a copy of their response to you. Penny Downs advised that a response was sent to you within 48 hours of receipt of your letter. I am sorry that this did not arrive with you. Penny has assured us that another copy of the letter has been sent to you, by registered post.

We hope this resolves the matter for you, and you can enjoy watching Arsenal with your son in the future.

Thank you for taking the time to contact us.

Yours sincerely,

Rachel Pallant
Supporter Relations Executive

10

Premier League
30 Gloucester Place   T +44 (0) 20 7864 9000
London W1U 8PL   F +44 (0) 20 7864 9001
premierleague.com   E info@premierleague.com

The Football Association Premier League Limited
Registered Office: 30 Gloucester Place, London, W1U 8PL. No. 2719699 England

if you're anything like me, and i know you are
because i can see you, then you will be wondering
what the clydebank fc squad of 1986 are doing
with themselves. after months of research i have
the answers:

CLYDEBANK FC 1986 - WHAT ARE THEY DOING NOW?

Mr Rob Paddon
Sales and Marketing Assistant
Exeter City Football Club
St James Park
Stadium Way
Exeter, EX4 6PX

Dear Mr Paddon,

Happy New Year to you and all involved at Exeter City Football Club! I am certain that 2010 will see Exeter City marching up that league table – I can just feel it in me water.

As a family we spend quite a lot of time in Tiverton (I won't bore you with the reasons why), and given its relative geographical proximity to Exeter we have developed something of a soft spot for your little club.

We head down there every month which is great fun and as my son Daniel (8) is a very promising young artist he just loves it. Daniel's passion for art knows no bounds and he has asked if it would be possible for him to paint portraits of your first team squad. Do you think that this is something you would be able to help arrange? I can assure you that he is really very good for his age. For example he recently painted a portrait of his piano teacher Mrs Telford and she thought it was so good that it now hangs proudly above the piano in her front room.

We feel that the portraits would look great in your club's boardroom, or could even be auctioned for charity if you felt that was the road you wanted to go down as a club.

I wasn't sure if you would be best placed to assist with this request, but I hope that you will be able to help my son's dream become reality. I look forward to hearing from you and thank you in advance for taking the time to consider our request.

Best Wishes,

Struan J. Marjoribanks

Exeter City Football Club
St James' Park
Exeter, Devon, EX4 6PX
Telephone: 01392 411243
Facsimile: 01392 413959
Email: enquiries@exetercityfc.co.uk

To Mr Marjoribanks

Thank you for very kind letter regarding your son Daniels Art proposal. It was a very interesting offer and something that we would be very interested in accepting. I am not sure to the logistics of this, however I can perhaps give you some guidance as to how this could happen.

I would suggest that we agree an image for your son to paint, perhaps from a photo or coming to the ground. We could then display the picture around the ground, and perhaps do a feature article in our programme/website etc. Unfortunately due to the hectic scheduling surrounding our players, it would be very difficult to get a player to sit for a portrait, perhaps a photo could be suitable?

If you would like to get back to me with more details of what your son would like to paint and where etc that would be great.

Kind Regards

Rob Paddon
Sales and Marketing Assistant
Exeter City Football Club

T: 01392 411243
E: rob.paddon@exetercityfc.co.uk
F: 01392 413959

13

Club Sponsor

www.exetercityfc.co.uk
Exeter City A.F.C. Ltd. Registered in England no. 97808

13th January 2010

Mr Rob Paddon
Sales and Marketing Assistant
Exeter City Football Club
St James Park
Stadium Way
Exeter, EX4 6PX

Dear Mr Paddon,

I cannot thank you enough for your undated letter which we received this morning. You have made Daniel's year and it is only the 13th of January!

Daniel was so excited when I read out your letter that he pulled on one of the curtains in his bedroom so hard that it snapped the curtain rail in two. Eight year old boys do seem to celebrate things in the most unusual of ways.

Daniel fully understands that due to their hectic and opulent lifestyles players are unable to sit for four or five hours after training in order to have their portrait painted by child. Daniel has therefore agreed to work from a photograph in the first instance.

When I asked Daniel what or who he would most like to paint he yelled out 'Troy Archibald-Henville' without even a millisecond's hesitation. Troy is Daniel's favourite Exeter City player as he fell in love with his name immediately upon hearing it and tells me that it is the perfect name for a 'swashbuckling defender.' I really don't know where he gets it from sometimes.

Would you therefore be able to send us a photograph of Troy from which Daniel can work? A close-up image of Troy's face would be best if you have such a thing.

If it is not possible to supply such a photograph of Troy then I'm sure Daniel will understand and he can pick someone else at the club like the manager or the chairman. However, here's hoping that there are no such hiccups and we cannot wait to hear from you.

Best Wishes,

Struan J. Marjoribanks

14

Exeter City Football Club

St James' Park
Exeter, Devon, EX4 6PX
Telephone: 01392 411243
Facsimile: 01392 413959
Email: enquiries@exetercityfc.co.uk

25/1/2010

To Mr Struan J.Majoribanks

Thank you for your very swift response and I am delighted that your son is so enthusiastic about Exeter City FC. Unfortunately today Troy Archibald-Henville returned to his parent club Tottenham Hotspurs FC. If your son desperately wishes to paint him then we would be delighted to see this.

However our recommendation is to perhaps paint fans favourite Adams Stansfield, I have enclosed a match day programme , and the preferred photo is on page 17. I hope your son would be happy to paint this, as we feel this is the best recent photo we have to send to you. As well as this we can then hopefully put this on the website etc

Should you have any other queries or concerns please do get back to me, and I would like to wish Daniel good luck with his painting!

Kind regards

Rob Paddon

Sales and Marketing Assistant
Exeter City FC

15

31st January 2010

Mr Rob Paddon
Sales and Marketing Assistant
Exeter City Football Club
St James Park
Stadium Way
Exeter, EX4 6PX

Dear Mr Paddon,

I cannot imagine the receipt of a letter producing greater mixed emotions than yours dated 25th of January. Heartfelt thanks for sending Daniel a copy of *The Grecian* which he was absolutely thrilled with, however, the news about Troy Archibald-Henville's departure from Exeter City has sadly had a profound effect on Daniel.

Neither of us were aware that football clubs had children, so to speak, and Troy Archibald-Henville going back to daddy has knocked poor Daniel for six. In fact, he just hasn't been himself since learning this news.

Over breakfast this morning I asked Daniel how he was feeling as he had spent around twenty minutes glumly swirling the milk about in his cornflakes with his spoon. Daniel picked up a pen and wrote 'G-U-T-T-E-D' in 3 down on the crossword in my Sunday newspaper. We have been wondering for a while now if Daniel could be mildly autistic.

As the day went on Daniel's mood thankfully improved and he admitted that he was up for the challenge of painting the portrait of Adam Stansfield which you yourself kindly suggested. Being more accustomed to the traditional head and shoulders portrait Daniel is slightly concerned about trying his hand at an action shot. He tells me that his intention is always to capture the inner essence of his subject and hopes this will still come through in his representation of the picture supplied.

Thanks again for providing a photograph from which Daniel can work. I'm sure that you will understand that Daniel strives for perfection and I have already seen some of his preliminary sketches which look rather promising. We therefore hope to be able to send you a portrait to be proud of in due course, and in the meantime may I wish yourself and all at Exeter City Football Club the kindest of regards from the Marjoribanks family.

Best Wishes,

Struan J. Marjoribanks

3rd March 2010

Mr Rob Paddon
Sales and Marketing Assistant
Exeter City Football Club
St James Park
Stadium Way
Exeter, EX4 6PX

Dear Mr Paddon,

Hokey Cokey - here's Adam Stansfield's portrait! Please also let me apologise for what must have felt to you like an inordinate delay. However, this was Daniel's eighteenth (yes 18th) attempt at the portrait such was his desire to get it just right.

I do hope that you will agree that it was worth the wait, and I probably mentioned previously that Daniel is a perfectionist. I hate to think how many hours in total Daniel spent on this project, and his other passion (archery) certainly suffered as a result. But Daniel knew this was an opportunity that required his full commitment and that is certainly what it got.

Thanks again for your encouragement and assistance, and we all look forward to hearing your thoughts on the portrait and what your plans are for it.

Best Wishes,

Struan J. Marjoribanks

Exeter City Football Club

St James' Park
Exeter, Devon, EX4 6PX
Telephone: 01392 411243
Facsimile: 01392 413959
Email: enquiries@exetercityfc.co.uk

Thursday 4th March 2010

To Mr S Marjoribanks,

Firstly thank you for your son Daniel's piece of artwork it was truly fantastic, and I was staggered at the quality, detail and shear likeness of Adam Stansfield. I took the piece to the training ground and it created quite a buzz amongst the players, with all of them very jealous of Adam, and his picture.

Adam would like to pass on his personal thanks for the artwork, and he took time out of his busy schedule to personally sign it. We have taken a digital copy of the artwork and we will be doing a feature article on the website shortly, in hope that perhaps children's art work could be regularly displayed.

Daniel should be very proud of his artwork, and I hope that by returning it signed he can put in a pride of place, and it will be something that he can treasure for a lifetime. I would like to thank Daniel again for all of his hard work that went into the painting and I hope he continues to enjoy following our team. I have enclosed last night's match programme as another gesture of thanks.

Kindest regards.

Rob Paddon

Rob Paddon
Exeter City FC

19

Club Sponsor

www.exetercityfc.co.uk
Exeter City A.F.C. Ltd. Registered in England no. 97808

To Daniel
Best Wishes

DJM

24th March 2010

Mr Rob Paddon
Sales and Marketing Assistant
Exeter City Football Club
St James Park
Stadium Way
Exeter, EX4 6PX

Dear Mr Paddon,

Wow! I have got one happy son Mr Paddon! What a kind gesture it was to have Stanny (as we have taken to calling Adam Stansfield) sign his own portrait, and the description of the training ground buzz which the portrait created had Daniel whooping with delight!

We are very grateful for Stanny's personal thanks, and Daniel is very keen to know what his exact words were when he saw the portrait as he likes to collect his subject's first impressions of his work. For example, I believe that his mother's words were 'gosh, that is truly wonderful,' while his piano teacher Mrs Telford said 'my goodness Daniel, it's like looking in a mirror.' Daniel tells me that it is important to record these reactions in order to gauge his ability at creating a likeness which meets the subject's approval.

We are also very excited at the prospect of the portrait featuring on Exeter City's website. Is that an internal thing or will it be available on the wider intranet?

Finally, thanks ever so much for the latest copy of The Grecian which was very gratefully received and thanks once again for all of your assistance – it quite literally would not have been possible without you.

Best Wishes,

Struan J. Marjoribanks

Exeter City Football Club

St James' Park
Exeter, Devon, EX4 6PX
Telephone: 01392 411243
Facsimile: 01392 413959
Email: enquiries@exetercityfc.co.uk

Friday 26th March 2010

To Mr S Marjoribanks,

I am delighted that Daniel has really enjoyed this art project, and we are delighted to have been part of it. I grabbed "Stanny" and although we can't remember his first words, he is genuinely delighted at the art work and was so grateful that Daniel took the time and effort to complete this fantastic piece.

With regards to our website the portrait will feature over the next few weeks at some point on www.exetercityfc.co.uk, depending on how busy our web team are, as you can appreciate with coming towards the end of the season they are very busy.

If Daniel would like to take part in any future projects we would be delighted for him to send us any art work. Thank you again for the artwork and I hope you enjoy the rest of the season.

Kindest regards.

Rob Paddon

Rob Paddon
Exeter City FC

22

my interview on 'the one show' once famous

the lovely matt: (smiling) so what was it that made you want

the lovely alex: (smiling) to write a book of prank

the lovely matt: (smiling) letters to football

the lovely alex: (smiling) clubs? (laughs)

me: (sneering) i don't really know

crew, presenters, gervais: (raucously) ha ha ha ha

me: (sneering) alex, when will you leave this show because you
think you're too good for it?

crew, the lovely matt, gervais: (raucously) ha ha ha ha

alex: (sheepishly) five weeks hence

Linvoy Primus
Head of Club Liaison
Portsmouth Football Club
Fratton Park
Frogmore Road
Portsmouth, Hants
PO4 8RA

Dear Mr Primus,

My son Daniel (8) informs me that Portsmouth FC is in grave financial peril, and you must forgive my ignorance in this regard. If Barcelona (the football club – not the city) disappeared off the face of the earth tomorrow, for example, I would find the story no more newsworthy than a child discovering a marshmallow resembling the face of our saviour Jesus Christ. I do apologise Mr Primus, as I may not be a football man, but Daniel, bless him, is a football boy.

Daniel regrets that he is unable to assist your club's financial plight due to his age. However, he has rather thoughtfully penned a Haiku as a testimonial to his favourite ever Portsmouth player – Nwankwo Kanu. He tells me the Haiku is a gesture of goodwill towards your club and he hopes that it can be used in a positive way. Indeed, he advises that if you are able to use the Haiku as a money-raiser in some way that he would be delighted and would not seek a penny in return – it is his gift to your club in its hour of need. We hope that you enjoy it.

Haiku For Nwankwo Kanu

You Nwankwo Kanu
How do you do what you do
In size fourteen shoe?

Every word here is true
You make the ball stick like glue
To size fourteen shoe

Worn red and worn blue
Beat a heart condition too
In size fourteen shoe

Best Wishes,

Struan J. Marjoribanks

NO RESPONSE

24

12th November 2009

Mr Paul McGowan
Ticket Office Manager
Brighton & Hove Albion Football Club
Ticket Office
128 Queens Road
Brighton
BN1 3WA

Dear Mr McGowan,

My son recently finished his dinner all by himself, and we have decided that a reward is in order. This may sound a little odd, but Daniel is 8 years old and has an extremely rare condition which makes him afraid of eating.

We asked Daniel what he would like to do in order to commemorate this milestone and he said that he would love to go to an English football match. After some persuasion Daniel's mother agreed that he could do this.

Daniel's favourite English football team is Brighton & Hove Albion. He liked the name and as a keen young ornithologist he plumped for your club due to the seagull on the club crest. Daniel informs me that the choice was between your club and Oldham Athletic (owl on crest) but as their name has food in it (ham) he opted for Brighton & Hove Albion.

As we are planning to attend a match soon I would like to know how much tickets will be in total for two adults and three children (we have reluctantly agreed to take two of Daniel's friends).

I very much look forward to hearing from you and receiving prices for the above. If you could also advise on methods of payment it would be greatly appreciated.

Best Wishes,

Struan J. Marjoribanks

25

BRIGHTON & HOVE ALBION
FOOTBALL CLUB

27th November 2009

Dear Struan,

Thank you for your letter. We are very pleased to hear of Daniel's progress and hope that he continues to do well. As a special reward we would like to offer him some free tickets. We're always pleased to hear from fans of the Albion regardless of how they came to support us - a budding Ornithologist is a certainly the most interesting reason that I've heard!

We would be pleased to offer Daniel x1 Adult and x1 Child complimentary tickets for any Home League Game (I have enclosed a fixture list for your perusal). In the Family Stand additional tickets will be from £23.50 for adults, £1 for under 10s and £4.50 for under 16s.

Please give us a call on 0845 496 1901 to organise which game you would like to come along to.

Kind regards

Paul

Paul McGowan

Ticket Office Manager
Brighton & Hove Albion FC

PS I have also enclosed a 'Gully's Gang' application form so tha Daniel can join up to our young supporters club.

Brighton & Hove Albion FC Ltd Tower Point, 44 North Rd, Brighton BN1 1YR | Tel 01273 695400 | Fax 01273 648179 | seagulls@bhafc.co.uk | www.seagulls.co.uk
Ticketline 0845 496 1901 | Merchandise Store 128 Queens Road, Brighton BN1 3WB 0845 4969 442 | Registered in England 81077 | VAT registration no 190 3035 89

IT First
KIT SPONSOR

26

2nd December 2009

Mr Paul McGowan
Ticket Office Manager
Brighton & Hove Albion Football Club
Ticket Office
128 Queens Road
Brighton
BN1 3WA

Dear Mr McGowan,

What a kind man you are! I was stunned by your generosity when your letter dated 27th November arrived *chez Marjoribanks*. As if the offer of membership to 'Gully's Gang' and the free fixture list were not sufficient you really tugged on the heartstrings with the offer of two complimentary tickets.

Daniel (8) had been eating exceptionally well since last I wrote (three Dairylea Triangles last night) and consequently Daniel's mother and I felt it only right to reward him sooner rather than later. We therefore treated Daniel to a metal detecting expedition on Saturday as this was something that he had always wanted to do. We may have trudged home with only a modest 19th century musket ball (well, that's what I told Daniel it was) to show for our troubles, but Daniel seemed to enjoy himself.

As Daniel has found a new hobby (our garden looks like an episode of Time Team!), would it be possible to give the free tickets to Alan and Joan Porter who live in nearby Rottingdean? I telephoned Alan last night and he said they were alright for the match against Huddersfield Town on January 23rd. If you could let me know if this is alright that would be greatly appreciated.

Thanks again for all of your warmth and generosity and I look forward to hearing from you soon. Here's hoping I can pass on good news to Alan and Joan.......

Best Wishes,

Struan J. Marjoribanks

END OF CORRESPONDENCE

28

30th January 2009

Mr Ron Gourlay
Chief Operating Officer
Chelsea Football Club
Stamford Bridge
London
SW6 1HS

Dear Mr Gourlay,

As marketing falls within your very broad remit I am hoping that you will be able to assist me with my inquiry.

We are forerunners in the luxury soup market and have been soup-makers to the stars for many years. Howard Keel, for example, was a very big fan of our soup and once even said as much in an interview on daytime television (I have the video somewhere).

Football is of course big business nowadays and I thought it may be an interesting and profitable venture to create an exclusive Chelsea FC soup. To my knowledge this kind of partnership is unprecedented.

My team of chefs have already begun working on the perfect Chelsea FC soup recipe and they believe that they are now very close. They have developed a smoked eel and fennel chowder (eel representing the club's London roots, and now a very fashionable fish as it happens, much like your football club). I have tasted the chowder and it certainly hits the back of the net, if I may say so myself.

We even have some ideas for the name of the soup – from Cheelsea Chowder to Stamford Broth, but this could be left up to the club, and could even perhaps be the subject of a fun naming competition for the fans, which in turn would raise the profile and awareness of the soup.

If given permission we would like to go into production in early April as our factory schedule permits this. Otherwise it may need to be nearer May. However, we naturally require the buy-in from your club for the soup to become an officially licensed product of Chelsea FC with the packaging containing the Chelsea crest etc.

Given the status of both of our organisations in our given fields this would seem, to me, like an ideal venture: two market leaders creating the first ever soup/football partnership.

I would be very interested to hear your thoughts on this proposal and then we can take it from there.

Best Wishes,

Struan J. Marjoribanks

29

**CHELSEA**FOOTBALL CLUB

Mr Struan J. Marjoribanks

4th February 2009

Dear Mr Marjoribanks

Thank you for your letter dated 30th January addressed to Ron Gourlay.

Your letter has been passed onto our head of catering who will be in contact with you should this be of interest.

Yours sincerely

Sheniz Osman-Jones
PA to Ron Gourlay – Chief Operating Officer
Chelsea Football Club
Tel: 0207 958 2824

30

Chelsea Football Club Ltd
Stamford Bridge
Fulham Road
London SW6 1HS

Tel 0871 984 1955
Fax 020 7381 4831
www.chelseafc.com
Registered No. 1965149
Registered Office Stamford Bridge

15th April 2009

Mr Simon Hunter
Head of Hospitality
Chelsea Football Club
Stamford Bridge
London, SW6 1HS

Dear Mr Hunter,

The lovely Ms Osman-Jones advised in her letter of 4th February 2009 that my letter (dated 30th January 2009) had been passed on to the 'head of catering,' which I hope to be yourself.

Since learning that my proposal had reached a fellow 'foodie' I have been waiting anxiously for news. Mail *can* go missing, but I felt sufficient time had elapsed to allow me to contact you for an update – particularly as our Spring factory schedule has since been firmed up.

In order to speed up the process I include the Chelsea FC smoked eel and fennel chowder recipe below. As you will see it has been penned in our factory chef Douglas Sinclair's own inimitable fashion, and I left it completely untouched for that certain *je-ne-sais-quoi*.

Smoked Eel and Fennel Chowder

1 pound smoked eel, skinned ('hold him down Cleatus')
1 large chopped fennel bulb (let there be light!)
2 tablespoons olive oil ('I yam what I yam. Ug, ug, ug')
6 cloves garlic, peeled and chopped (breath, vampires, the French.....)
2 large onions, peeled and chopped (tissues anyone???)
1 jalapeno pepper, seeded and chopped finely (I'm feeling hot, hot, hot!)
4 tomatoes, chopped (canned tomatoes are OK if you got monged and forgot to buy fresh)
1 pound potatoes, diced and cooked until tender in fish stock (optional, but do chuck 'em in)
1 cup seafood stock (if you don't have this just use vegetable stock, no actually just get this)
1 cup double cream (it's so bad, but it's sooo damn good!)
Salt and pepper to taste (go easy on the salt Sport)
Garnish: finely chopped parsley ('aw, in't that nice? Sharon, I said in't that nice. Well in't it?')

Preparation

Heat the oil in a large pot and stir in garlic, onions, and jalapeno pepper and sauté until soft. Add the tomato pieces and cook down over medium heat (8 mins). Toss in the eel and fennel, covering and steaming for 2 mins. Remove cover and let stew gently for 5 mins until the eel is just done. Pour in the stock and bring to a boil. Stir in the cooked potatoes (optional) and return to a simmer. Stir in cream. When the chowder is simmering, it is ready to serve. Flake the eel into the soup. Ladle the soup into bowls and garnish with chopped parsley.

Mr Hunter, would you do me the honour of having your top chef make you a bowl of this rather fine soup? I'm very keen to hear your thoughts on not only the soup itself, but also how well you feel it mirrors the stature, style and very essence of your club. I would like to thank you in advance for your assistance with this matter, and I look forward to hearing from you.

Best Wishes,

Struan J. Marjoribanks

31

END OF CORRESPONDENCE

my **vivid** dream: 15th august 2007

me: so your name is karl-heinz rummenigge and you
                                 would like us to manufacture an apricot soup?

karl-heinz rummenigge: yes, mass production for the german market

me: sounds great, i'll speak to our head chef

me: so, douglas, i want an apricot soup for the germans

douglas sinclair: no can do struan, i have my professional integrity
                                 as head soup chef to think about

me: oh bother

me: bad news i'm afraid mr rummenigge — my head chef
                                 just will not make an apricot soup

karl-heinz rummenigge: then have him disposed of immediately

me: oh bother! i'm glad this is just a dream

3rd October 2008

Mr Ted Hennessey
Financial Director
Peterborough United Football Club
London Road Stadium
London Road
Peterborough
Cambridgeshire, PE2 8AL

Dear Mr Hennessey,

The town of Peterborough, and indeed Cambridgeshire, has remained close to my heart after spending many unforgettable family holidays there as a boy. I have continued this tradition by taking my son Daniel (8) down to the 'Borough (as we call it) as often as possible during the school holidays. The people are always so warm and friendly, and Daniel generally feels that he makes more friends in a fortnight in Peterborough than he has in 8 years up yonder.

Anyhoo, my letter is of a business nature. Our love affair with your town has naturally resulted in Peterborough United FC becoming the football club of choice in the Marjoribanks household, and after a rather successful career in the soup industry I am looking for a way to mark my forthcoming retirement in style.

Mr Hennessey, my proposal is that in return for a sizeable monetary donation to the club that the main stand of the London Road Stadium be renamed The Struan J. Marjoribanks Stand. This would naturally give my family immense pride, but more importantly it would inject some capital into the club at this time of financial uncertainty.

If the club is considering renaming the main stand after one of the club's great figures of yesteryear (as seems to be *de rigueur* these days) then I will fully understand. What I would then propose to do is to up the stakes a little in return for the stadium being renamed Marjoribanks Park - this would then allow you to rename the stands as you see fit.

My family and I eagerly await your response regarding this proposal, and we sincerely hope that as Financial Director you urge the club's board to seize this opportunity.

Best Wishes,

Struan J. Marjoribanks

33

PETERBOROUGH UNITED FOOTBALL CLUB

London Road Stadium, London Road, Peterborough, PE2 8AL **t:** +44 (0)1733 563947 **f:** +44 (0)1733 344140 **e:** info@theposh.com

7 October, 2008

Mr Struan J Marjoribanks

Dear Mr Marjoribanks

Naming Rights

Thank you for your kind and interesting letter in regard to potential Naming Rights at London Road. I am also very glad to hear that Daniel is enjoying his visits to our club and enjoying the atmosphere.

We would of course be interested in talking to you about your proposal and would suggest that we arrange a preliminary meeting to introduce ourselves and discuss the options.

I would be more than happy to travel to a meeting place of your convenience initially and then invite you to London Road to progress and hopefully finalise any agreed arrangements.

Thank you again for your time and interest and I await your further response.

Yours sincerely

Bob Symns
Chief Executive Officer

34

www.theposh.com

Full members of the Football Association. Associate Members of the
Football League. Registered in England no. 290803. VAT No. 120167319.

17th October 2008

Mr Bob Symns
Chief Executive Officer
Peterborough United Football Club
London Road Stadium
London Road
Peterborough
Cambridgeshire, PE2 8AL

Dear Mr Symns,

Many thanks for your encouraging letter, suitably entitled 'Naming Rights,' dated 7th October.
Please excuse the delay in responding to you, but I have only just returned from a shark
fishing trip in Namibia, and boy is there good sport to be had in them waters!

It would be a pleasure to meet with you to discuss my proposal and I greatly appreciate your
offer of travelling to meet me. However, I am well aware just how busy you are, and I
therefore wish to make this as simple as possible for you.

The next few weeks are extremely busy for me as it happens. Tomorrow I am flying out to Oz
at short notice as Cousin Bryce requires the kind of financial assistance which cannot wait
any longer for fear of what could happen to his family if he fails to pay off his debts. Please
don't ask Mr Symns! Every family has a black sheep I'm sure: it is just unfortunate that ours
lives on the other side of the world and never seems to learn from his mistakes.

Immediately 'pon my return it is a week of intensive restructuring and pre-retirement
arrangements at the factory, and then it's back to Namibia for another week's sun and big
game fishing afore the festive season is upon us. Once you've caught your first Bronzy (the
Namibian bronze whaler shark) the thought of fly fishing locally, even against the stunning
backdrop of Scotland's golden autumnal scenery, just doesn't get this old fellow's juices
flowing like it used to.

Due to our busy schedules I feel that it might be an idea to gauge if we are on the same page
regarding naming rights before arranging a meeting. Are you able to give me a rough
'ballpark' figure of the kind of investment which would be required in return for the renaming of
the main stand at London Road Stadium?

God knows soup has been good to me, but it has not provided me with the kind of wealth
where vast sums of money can be spent on football clubs or mindless trans-global races in
disgustingly expensive sports cars. I therefore do not view investment in Peterborough
United as a sustainable or continuous thing. No, I simply view this transaction as me
donating a sum of money in return for my name being emblazoned across your main stand.
Vain? Shallow? Egotistical? Yes, perhaps it is all of those things, but that is the result of
being *numero uno* in soup for many years.

I look forward to hearing from you, so that on my return we can hopefully get things moving.

Best Wishes,

35

Struan J. Marjoribanks

PETERBOROUGH UNITED FOOTBALL CLUB

London Road Stadium, London Road, Peterborough, PE2 8AL t: +44 (0)1733 563947 f: +44 (0)1733 344140 e: info@theposh.com

17 December, 2008

Mr Struan J Marjoribanks

Dear Struan

Thank you for your recent correspondence and I am glad you arrived back in one piece after your latest adventure, It will be interesting to hear the detail.

February sounds fine to me for our meeting and I am glad to say that I have no allergies of which I am aware and I enjoy most foods !

I hope you and the family have a wonderful Christmas and best wishes for the New Year.

Regards

Bob Symns
Chief Executive Officer

38

4th February 2009

Mr Bob Symns
Chief Executive Officer
Peterborough United Football Club
London Road Stadium
London Road
Peterborough
Cambridgeshire, PE2 8AL

Dear Mr Symns,

Happy New Year to you! Isn't 2009 in danger of running away from us already?

You know, it was only when Andrea woke me the other morning and wished me a 'happy February' that I realised that I had better phone the wife and ask her to prepare one of the guest rooms for your visit.

Are you still in the mood for some soup tasting? Bring it on Daddy-O! We should have a lot of fun. I was asked to give a presentation at a recent soup conference and used a couple of my son Daniel's (8) latest soup jokes (he collects them bless him):

Child: Mummy, mummy what's a vampire?
Mother: Shut up and eat your soup before it clots.

What's the difference between roast beef and pea soup? Anyone can roast beef.

Somebody complimented the cannibal cook on his soup and he replied "It's all relatives."

I thought those were rather good for an eight year old, but I doubt he actually made them up, despite Daniel's claims that he did. Have you got any good football jokes?

How's business? I'm not ashamed to admit that even I have been feeling the pinch recently. For example, I had no alternative but to reduce my driver's hours, which being a father of four he objected strongly to. As a result he is now also peeling carrots on Tuesday and Wednesday afternoons.

Has your club been feeling the effects of the so-called Credit Crunch? Are attendances down? Are less pies being eaten? Are players moaning even more than normal?

I know that times are tough right now, and I wouldn't want to assume that you will be making the journey in the current inclement financial climate, so please let me know how you are placed.

In the meantime I trust that you are keeping well, and I look forward to hearing from you.

Best Wishes,

Struan J. Marjoribanks   39

PETERBOROUGH UNITED FOOTBALL CLUB

London Road Stadium, London Road, Peterborough, PE2 8AL **t:** +44 (0)1733 563947 **f:** +44 (0)1733 344140 **e:** info@theposh.com

20 March, 2009

Mr Struan J Marjoribanks

Dear Struan

As usual it was good to hear from you and the jokes were an added bonus … well done Daniel.

Business here at Peterborough United is good with the team pushing hard for automatic promotion to the Championship, however, we are very aware of the financial climate and would completely understand if you wish to defer your interest in any sponsorship at this particular moment in time. Should you wish to continue I would be more than happy to come and meet you at your convenience.

Regards

Bob Symns
Chief Executive Officer

40

8th April 2009

Mr Bob Symns
Chief Executive Officer
Peterborough United Football Club
London Road Stadium
London Road
Peterborough
Cambridgeshire, PE2 8AL

Dear Mr Symns,

Lovely to hear from you as always Bob. I am of course referring to your letter dated 20th March 2009.

It has taken me a little longer than usual to respond due to spending the last couple of weeks trying in earnest to learn a foreign language. In the end I had to give up.

I was delighted to read that Peterborough United are doing so well and are currently in contention for promotion. Our factory team are also enjoying considerable success at the moment and had a very encouraging 2-2 draw recently against the much-feared McGarvey Bakery.

Incidentally I passed on your kind words to Daniel regarding his jokes and he was what Scousers in particular often seem to describe as 'made up.' You are a kind man Mr Symns.

Daniel promised that by way of thanks he would make up a Peterborough United joke for me to include in this letter, but with no gag forthcoming he very sheepishly admitted defeat over breakfast this morning. This only adds weight to my suspicions regarding the authenticity of 'his' soup jokes.

Your understanding regarding my deferment of sponsorship interest for the time-being was also greatly appreciated. I'd hate for you to think for one minute that I was scraubling you about (as we say up here), and your letter therefore meant a lot to me.

Please do keep in touch, however, and let me know how Peterborough United's push for promotion goes. I have to admit that I have slightly mixed feelings in that regard, because if promotion is secured then the renaming of the main stand would presumably cost more next season than it would have this. That, I suppose, is what a dear friend of mine describes as *just the way the jobby splatters*.

Do take care Mr Symns, and I look forward to our continued communication.

Best Wishes,

41

Struan J. Marjoribanks

END OF
CORRESPONDENCE

25th January 2010

Mr Trevor Brock
Secretary
Havant & Waterlooville Football Club
2 Betula Close
Waterlooville
Hampshire, PO7 8EJ

Dear Mr Brock,

CONGRATULATIONS!

I have just been reading all about your club's heroics in the 2007/8 FA Cup and was dumbfounded when I read that in the 4th round of the cup you were in front twice against Liverpool FC before eventually losing 5-2.

Quite, quite amazing!

I can't believe that nobody told me about it sooner. Well done to all concerned.

Best Wishes,

Struan J. Marjoribanks

42

somebody asked me eight years ago if i knew what
the guilty pleasures of the 1986 rangers fc squad
were. they said winning games wasn't one of them.
i embarked on a long voyage of discovery and here
are the answers:

RANGERS FC 1986 - WHAT ARE THEIR GUILTY PLEASURES?

31st October 2008

Mr Stuart Ryan
Director of Marketing
West Ham United Football Club
Boleyn Ground
Green Street
London, E13 9AZ

Dear Mr Ryan,

As you get older you find yourself eye-balling life's cruel malevolence in a way that would have been unthinkable in your younger years, don't you find? I certainly do.

As a successful businessman now nearing retirement I am in a position to question things which I was previously unaware even had questions to be asked of them. My first wife worked in a charity shop on Saturday mornings and she taught me plenty about the need for us all to find a little humanitarian spirit. It is in this regard that I hope you can assist me.

Mr Ryan, I am very concerned about the manner in which many of our Western luxuries are manufactured. For example, can you be sure that West Ham United Football Club's team kit and match balls have not been manufactured in Indian sweatshops? Would you be happy for your star striker to score a goal using a football which was sewn together in the dark by a semi-blind six-year-old Indian child whose soul has been vandalised by a multi-national sporting goods company?

I do not need to remind you that you are very much in the public eye, and that your players are seen as role models by young people such as my son Daniel (8). I therefore hope that you will agree that it is vitally important that your club is not indirectly supporting child slave labour by using and endorsing products made in the most appallingly inhumane conditions.

Your club is very dear to my heart, and as such I pray that it cares for the plight of those less fortunate than ourselves, and perhaps takes a stand where other football clubs dare not. Football is, after all, the people's game.

I look forward to hearing your thoughts on this, and I hope for reassuring news.

Best Wishes,

Struan J. Marjoribanks

44

November 15th 2008

Dear Mr Marjoribanks,

Thank you for your letter dated October 31st and your comments concerning
the ethical responsibility that West Ham United FC has regards the player's
kits.

In order to respond to your enquiry I contacted Carole Greenwood, Director
of Corporate Social Responsibility at Umbro who supply player's kit. You will
probably be aware that Umbro are owned by Nike who also supply the
match balls you refer to. I have enclosed her response with this letter and I
hope that this provides some reassurance for you that the matters you raise
are a priority for Umbro, Nike and West Ham United FC.

Thank you for taking the time to forward your feedback to us and for your
continued support of the Club.

Yours sincerely,

Tam Lever
Head of Retail
West Ham United FC

45

WEST HAM UNITED FOOTBALL CLUB PLC

REGISTERED OFFICE: BOLEYN GROUND, GREEN STREET, UPTON PARK, LONDON, E13 9AZ
Telephone: 020 8548 2748 Facsimile: 020 8548 2758 www.whufc.com Registered in England No. 66516

As a brand, we aim to bring the same level of passion and commitment to the area of the Compliance aspect of our Corporate Social Responsibility program , that we do to football.

As part of Nike's recent acquisition of Umbro we are currently undergoing a significant review of our business strategy, policies and processes which includes Umbro's CR program. The outcome will be aligned with Nike's Code of Conduct and supporting standards and policies.

That said, the complexity and depth of the issues facing a global supply chain are a challenge to all brands, including Umbro.
However, we take all reported non-compliance issues very seriously and work to research and validate all findings before moving on to developing long-term, sustainable corrective actions.
Part of that commitment includes ongoing collaboration and open dialogue with all stakeholders. We are committed to participating in forums, either at the global or national level, undertaken by these groups.

Umbro has a CSR monitoring team based in the UK and Asia who work closely with contract factories to identify, remediate and monitor against our Code of Conduct. We are a member of Fair Labor Association (FLA) and World Federation of Sporting Goods Industry (WFSGI) and are actively working alongside Nike, in collaboration with other sporting goods brands, on shared remediation and monitoring plans where our supply bases cross over.

As Umbro's appointed CSR Director, I hope that I have been able to give some reassurances that Umbro does take Corporate Responsibility within its supply chain extremely seriously.

Regards

Carole Greenwood
Director of CSR
Umbro.

46

UMBRO INTERNATIONAL LIMITED
UMBRO HOUSE, LAKESIDE, CHEADLE ROYAL BUSINESS PARK
CHEADLE, CHESHIRE SK8 3GQ
TEL: +44 (0)161 492 2000   FAX: +44 (0)161 492 2001
SALES OFFICE: +44 (0)161 492 2222
REGISTERED No. 198168 ENGLAND

23rd November 2008

Ms Carole Greenwood
Director of CSR
Umbro
Umbro House
Lakeside
Cheadle Royal Business Park
Cheadle
Cheshire, 5K8 3GQ

Dear Ms Greenwood,

Tam Lever, West Ham United's Head of Retail, was kind enough to send on to me your letter regarding Umbro's Corporate Social Responsibility program after I had written to him seeking reassurances that his club was not indirectly supporting the exploitation of children in Asia and other poor places.

Naturally I was delighted to read that Umbro is committed to the fair treatment of workers in their factories, and was relieved to read about the membership of the FLA and WFSGI.

However, I recently read on a human rights internet forum concerned with the manufacture of sporting goods that grave concerns abound regarding a toxic resin which may still be used in the manufacture of goalkeeper's gloves. I read one horror story of a teenage Indian factory worker (Anil) being blinded in one eye by the ghastly stuff! A couple of Anil's friends had apparently coated the frames of his spectacles in the resin as a practical joke, and so toxic was it that it left him blind in one eye.

As a precautionary measure, and as a matter of principal, I have stopped my son Daniel (8) from wearing his goalkeeper's gloves until I receive confirmation that these claims regarding the resin are unfounded. If you were able to provide a response on this issue it would be greatly appreciated as Daniel has been teased (nay tormented) for the last couple of weeks for wearing gardening gloves while keeping goal for his school team.

By all accounts Daniel let in two 'granny's growlers' (howlers) in his last match as a result of having no grip with the gardening gloves – one being a tame pass-back from his own defender which slipped from his grasp and trundled through his legs for an own goal. Mr Hastings, the teacher who runs the school team, had his work cut out to prevent Daniel from being lynched at the final whistle!

Your assistance with this matter would be greatly appreciated: not only by myself but also by Daniel who has subsequently lost his place in the school team to Robert Millard who he says is like one of those obese American children that you often see.

I look forward to hearing your thoughts on this and pray for further good news.

Best Wishes,

Struan J. Marjoribanks   47

5th January 2009

Mr Tam Lever
Head of Retail
West Ham United Football Club
Boleyn Ground
Green Street
London, E13 9AZ

Dear Mr Lever,

Happy New Year to you! I hope that 2009 brings you everything that you hope for and more (a trophy for West Ham would be nice, wouldn't it?). Have you made any New Year resolutions? I make the same one every year - to stop overfeeding our cat Smokey - but alas I can never stick to it.

You may remember that I wrote to you at the end of October regarding my concerns surrounding the inhumane working conditions widely reported to be found in the manufacture of sporting goods. You were kind enough to follow up with Carole Greenwood at Umbro, and forwarded me on her neatly worded, if somewhat vague response.

I subsequently wrote to Ms Greenwood on 23rd November to ask her specifically about a toxic resin rumoured to be used in the manufacture of goalkeeping gloves. An Indian boy is allegedly now blind, and I have stopped my son Daniel (8) from wearing his Umbro goalkeeping gloves as a result. Despite advising Ms Greenwood that my actions had resulted in Daniel being dropped from the school team (he has since regained his place due to his replacement's woeful incompetence) she has so far failed to respond.

Are you aware of the hazardous resin supposedly found in goalkeeping gloves? Would you perhaps be able to follow this up with the goalkeeping department at the club to establish if they have been made aware of the potential dangers contained in the tools of their trade?

If one of the West Ham goalkeepers is short-sighted, for example, and they adjust the position of a troublesome contact lens using a gloved hand then this could have disastrous consequences if the rumours are in fact true.

Naturally I would not wish to be seen as a scaremonger, and there may of course be no truth in these rumours, but we can never be too careful. I would therefore greatly appreciate it if you could put my mind at ease by confirming that the goalkeeping department are aware of these potential dangers and only use and endorse goalkeeping gloves made with safe materials.

I look forward to hearing from you, and as always, up the Hammers!

Best Wishes,

Struan J. Marjoribanks

48

12 January, 2009

Mr Struan Marjoribanks

Dear Mr Majoribanks

Thank you for your letter dated 26th November.
Please accept my apologies for the delay in responding to you.

Thank you for your follow up letter. As you point out there are many areas where responsible companies need to remain vigilant.

In addition to the earlier information I sent you, you may also want to go to the website (www.nikeresponsibility.com/rsl) and review some of the chemical standards that Nike Inc. (which includes Umbro) impose upon our supply chain. As you will see, we have high standards as we are committed to protect the consumer, the worker, and the environment.

Finally, I would like to reassure further that no Umbro goal keeper gloves in our ranges are produced in India.

I hope the info I have given you and made available has been able to assist in eliminating your concerns about Umbro products. We value your good opinion and we hope that you will continue to trust Umbro products for your son and others you care about.
I would also like to offer, as a goodwill gesture to your son, a pair of Umbro goal keeper gloves and a West Ham goal keeper jumper. Hopefully this may go some way to compensating your son for having to wear gardening gloves and subsequently losing his place. ...."Look out Robert Millard" ...Daniel is on his way back !

Kind Regards

Carole Greenwood

Director of CSR

49

UMBRO INTERNATIONAL LIMITED
UMBRO HOUSE, LAKESIDE, CHEADLE ROYAL BUSINESS PARK
CHEADLE, CHESHIRE SK8 3GQ
TEL: +44 (0)161 492 2000   FAX: +44 (0)161 492 2001
SALES OFFICE: +44 (0)161 492 2222
REGISTERED No. 198168 ENGLAND

daniel (8) in west ham
goalkeeping jersey and umbro gloves

29th January 2009

Ms Carole Greenwood
Director of CSR
Umbro
Umbro House
Lakeside
Cheadle Royal Business Park
Cheadle
Cheshire, 5K8 3GQ

Dear Ms Greenwood,

I cannot thank you enough for your letter dated 12th January 2009, and for your extremely kind gesture of sending Daniel (8) a pair of 'awesome' goalkeeping gloves (Daniel's description) and a 'fabby doo' West Ham goalkeeping jersey (my description). Daniel is absolutely thrilled with the jersey too, but kids just don't say things like 'fabby doo' any more, do they?

Daniel had taken the whole gardening gloves saga (now commonly known as Millardgate) so badly that he had appeared to ration the number of words that he would say to me each day to no more than ten. I am delighted to report that your generosity has put an end to all of that carry on, and I can hardly keep him quiet about 'the kind Umbro lady' (you).

Your confirmation that Umbro goalkeeping gloves are not made in India provided great relief to me, and it just proves that you can't always believe what you read. I am overjoyed that there is no Anil, or at least if there is that he isn't blind, or if by chance there is and that he is blind then it is nothing to do with goalkeeping gloves (I hope you followed that).

I can admit when I'm wrong, Ms Greenwood, and with the benefit of hindsight I can see that I was perhaps a little too hasty with the gardening gloves.

I am pleased to inform you that Daniel had actually already regained his place in the team (even with the handicap of the gardening gloves) due to the podgy Robert Millard being a particularly incompetent goalkeeper even for that age group. Daniel jokes that Robert Millard couldn't catch a cold, but if cream cakes were used instead of a ball that he would probably go on to play for England. I thought that was rather good for an eight year old, don't you?

Also, Robert Millard apparently wet himself during one game which opened the door somewhat for Daniel's return.

Many thanks once again for all of your assistance with my concerns and queries. You have been extremely helpful which has been greatly appreciated; not to mention the comfort it has given me to discover that Umbro (and indeed Nike) take human rights as seriously as I do.

It would be remiss of me not to also pass on Daniel's thanks for your generous gifts which he advises me have made him the envy of all his friends, and have made Robert Millard as sick as a parrot! (Get in there!). Finally, I would like to wish you and everyone at Umbro a happy, responsible and peaceful 2009.

Best Wishes,

Struan J. Marjoribanks

51

END OF CORRESPONDENCE

my appearance on 'match of the day' once famous

the lovely gary: (smiling) he's bonkers, he wrote a book of
                     prank letters to football clubs........but not
                     spurs.   why not spurs?

me: (with pure hate in my eyes)   i don't really
                     know

the lovely gary: ha ha, see what i mean.   we've just watched
                     bolton's draw with my old team......spurs.   what
                     did you make of it?

me: sorry, i wasn't watching, i was drawing this
                     picture of a child harpooning a manta ray

the lovely gary: (grinning as smugly as a human can) bonkers

WEST OF SCOTLAND

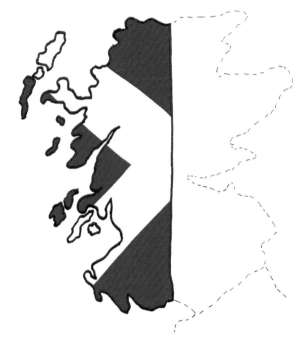

- Celtic
- Dumbarton
- Ayr United
- Morton

struan's west of scotland facts

throughout the bronze age it was common to be buried alive as punishment for disagreeing with an older person

if nobody had ever emigrated from this area there would currently be three to a bed

six archaeology students went for a pub lunch in cumbernauld in 1984 and were never seen again - their plates of pie, beans and chips, and their pints of lager were left eerily untouched on the table at which they had been sitting

represents the overuse (and misuse) of the phrase 'anyone for tennis?' whenever anyone is seen carrying a racquet of any description

Mr Chris McCart
Head of Youth Development
Celtic Football Club
Celtic Park
Glasgow
G40 3RE

Dear Mr McCart,

Many congratulations on attaining the lofty position of Head of Youth Development! Best of luck with it – and I trust you are acutely aware of the responsibility bestowed upon you when one considers the wealth of young talent that this club has produced over the seasons, nay centuries.

I would imagine that one of the biggest problems which you face from the youngsters these days is attitude. They know being a professional footballer can bring them the money, the attractive women and the fast cars, but perhaps they don't always appreciate the hard work required to succeed in the game and get their hands on those wonderful things. We both desperately want Celtic's youngsters to keep their feet on the ground and make the most of the opportunity that you and your colleagues work so hard to furnish them with.

Does all that sound familiar? Well, this is where I feel that I can help you, and in a *quid pro quo* style arrangement, perhaps you can help me too.

I am a businessman Mr McCart, and soup is my business. What I propose is that we introduce a work experience programme at my soup factory for the Celtic youngsters. Such an initiative will teach them not only the value of money (I will pay them the going factory rate), but it will also highlight to them where they could end up if they don't work sufficiently hard at their game. A simple but brilliant idea don't you think?

We could probably take five boys on at a time and put them on the factory floor for let's say two week blocks – this should be plenty time to enable them to reassess their lives. Also, don't worry, the boys will be provided with a full health and safety induction and all the necessary protective factory clothing.

From my perspective our soup productivity rate should increase substantially given the extra numbers on the floor, but most importantly you will get back more focussed and grounded young men after their experience. Surely that has to benefit Celtic Football Club in the long term.

If you could let me know your thoughts on this proposal I would be very grateful, and then we will be able to get the ball rolling (and the soup pouring).

Best Wishes,

Struan J. Marjoribanks

54

5 September 2008

Mr Struan J Marjoribanks

Dear Struan

Thank you for your letter dated 26 July regarding work experience for our youth players, and please accept my sincere apologies for not replying to you sooner. Thank you also for your kind words regarding my appointment as Head of Youth, a challenge which I am looking forward to.

Whilst I think that your idea of accepting our youth players on work experience at your soup factory has some worth, we are unfortunately not in a position to move forward with this at the present time. However, I will pass your letter on to our Education & Welfare Officer to keep on file should we wish to progress with this in the future.

Kind regards

Chris McCart
Head of Youth

Celtic F.C. Limited Football Department   Telephone 0871 226 1888   Facsimile 0141 551 4342
Celtic Park Glasgow G40 3RE   International Enquiries +44 871 226 1888   www.celticfc.net

Celtic F.C. Limited is a subsidiary of Celtic plc. Registered Office: Celtic Park, Glasgow G40 3RE Registered Number 227604 Scotland Vat Reg No 661 0295 62.

16th September 2008

Ms Elaine McCulloch
Education and Welfare Officer
Celtic Football Club
Celtic Park
Glasgow, G40 3RE

Dear Ms McCulloch,

I received a lovely letter yesterday from Head of Youth Chris McCart in which he advises that he has forwarded on to you my letter of 26th July 2008.

My housekeeper Mrs Adams read out Mr McCart's letter to me as I had cut myself quite badly shaving just as it was posted through my door. I was simply thrilled to hear that Mr McCart had passed the details over to you in order that we might proceed with our work experience programme.

I understand that Mr McCart is unable to release some of his youngsters at this time, but the prospect of their arrival in the near future has given everybody at the factory such a lift.

Is it possible for you to advise when we are likely to receive our first batch of boys? Also, will you be able to put a word in with Mr McCart so that there are a couple of genuine stars of the future involved in the scheme? It would be a dream to watch on in my retirement as a youngster I had trained to prep carrots scores in the Champions League for example.

If we can firm up the dates then I can order the necessary protective clothing and vegetables.

I look forward to hearing from you.

Best Wishes,

Struan J. Marjoribanks

5 September 2008

Mr Struan J Marjoribanks

████████████
████████
████████████
████████

Dear Struan

Thank you for your letter dated 26 July regarding work experience for our youth players, and please accept my sincere apologies for not replying to you sooner. Thank you also for your kind words regarding my appointment as Head of Youth, a challenge which I am looking forward to.

Whilst I think that your idea of accepting our youth players on work experience at your soup factory has some worth, we are unfortunately not in a position to move forward with this at the present time. However, I will pass your letter on to our Education & Welfare Officer to keep on file should we wish to progress with this in the future.

Kind regards

Chris McCart
Head of Youth

Celtic F.C. Limited Football Department
Celtic Park Glasgow G40 3RE

Telephone 0871 226 1888
International Enquiries +44 871 226 1888

Facsimile 0141 551 4342
www.celticfc.net

Celtic F.C. Limited is a subsidiary of Celtic plc. Registered Office: Celtic Park, Glasgow G40 3RE. Registered Number 223604 Scotland. Vat Reg No. 653 0293 52.

15 October 08

Mr Struan Marjoribanks

████████████████
████████
████████████
████████

Dear Struan

Re: Work Experience

Thank you for your letter dated 16 September, addressed to Elaine McCulloch regarding work experience for our Youth Players at your factory. Unfortunately there seems to have been some misunderstanding in relation to the letter we sent to you on 5 September (copy enclosed).

As you may appreciate we get many requests from Company's like yours and from other such organisations looking to take our youngsters on work experience. All such requests are passed on to our Education & Welfare Officer, Mr Brian Meehan for consideration. In respect of your particular request, both myself and Mr Meehan felt that we were unable to proceed with this but would keep your letter on file, as we do with all such requests, should circumstances change. Therefore we have no plans either at the present time or in the foreseeable future to send you any of our Youth Players for work experience.

We are extremely sorry for any confusion this may have caused and for any disappointment that both yourself and your staff may feel as a result.

Kind regards

Chris McCart
Head of Youth

END OF
CORRESPONDENCE

58

Celtic F.C. Limited Football Department
Celtic Park Glasgow G40 3RE

Telephone 0871 226 1888
International Enquiries +44 871 226 1888

Facsimile 0141 551 4342
www.celticfc.net

Celtic F.C. Limited is a subsidiary of Celtic plc, Registered Office Celtic Park, Glasgow G40 3RE, Registered Number 223504 Scotland. Vat Reg No 653 0293 52

26th August 2008

Mr Stevie Hunter
Kit Man
Dumbarton Football Club
Strathclyde Homes Stadium
Castle Road
Dumbarton, G82 1JJ

Dear Mr Hunter,

I have a query for you after attending the match at your stadium on 23rd August against Stenhousemuir, and I would be very grateful for any assistance you can offer.

Don't be cross with me but I am a Stenhousemuir fan and have been for many years. My grandfather fought beside a wonderful gentleman by the name of Bud Milligan in the War, and Bud was such a passionate and loyal fan of Stenhousemuir that it had a profound effect on my grandfather. Stenhousemuir therefore became my grandfather's team and this love for the club has been passed down through the generations in the Marjoribanks family. My son Daniel (8) classes himself as a Real Madrid fan first and a Stenhousemuir fan second, but you know what kids are like.

As you will remember from the game - if you weren't back in the changing room attending to further kit duties - Stenhousemuir scored a last gasp winner. In the ensuing commotion I somehow managed to lose a shoe, and this is where I am hoping that you can perhaps help me.

Please don't think for one minute that I am suggesting that you would be responsible for a 'lost and found' section at the stadium should one exist. However, my wife took five minutes out at the surgery to have a look at your club's 'webs site' and she felt that perhaps you would be the office bearer closest to a 'lost and found' section should one exist.

The shoe is a size ten black brogue for the left foot. The writing on the inner sole has worn away through age and I cannot remember the name of the manufacturer – however, the lace is extremely frayed and this should hopefully assist in identifying the shoe should there be more than one. There may also be a barely noticeable speckle of yellow paint on the shoe as I have examined the right shoe which has just such markings (I must have worn the shoes while painting Daniel's bedroom last year).

Being on such a high after the thrilling end to the game it was not until I was back on our bus and on our way home that I realised the shoe was missing. I would be eternally grateful if you could look into this matter for me and advise if my shoe has been handed in. I am very willing to pay for the shoe to be posted back to me should you recover it.

I look forward to hearing from you and pray for good news.

Best Wishes,

Struan J. Marjoribanks

Dumbarton Football Club
Strathclyde Homes Stadium
Castle Road
Dumbarton
G81 1JJ

Tel: 01389 762 569
Fax: 01389 762 629
Web: www.dumbartonfootballclub.com

Struan J Marjoribanks

1st September 2008

Dear Mr Marjoribanks

Thank you for your letter dated 26th August 2008. Despite a thoroug search we regret to advise that your missing left shoe has not been found.

Yours sincerely

Rowan Scott
Administrator

60

Ms Rowan Scott
Administrator
Dumbarton Football Club
Strathclyde Homes Stadium
Castle Road
Dumbarton, G82 1JJ

Dear Ms Scott,

Many, many thanks for your short yet informative letter dated 1st September 2008. I am very grateful to you for conducting a thorough search for my missing shoe and I was devastated to read that your efforts were fruitless.

My Auntie Jessie will be 90 soon and there will be quite a shindig (venue as yet unknown) to mark such a remarkable achievement: Auntie Jessie will be the oldest Marjoribanks for seven generations! I'm sure you will understand that my black brogues are very much required for that occasion.

I can almost hear you saying 'go and buy another pair Mr Marjoribanks, the shops still sell black brogues.' But I have an extremely broad foot you see Ms Scott, and I have found it nigh on impossible to buy shoes in the last five years. In fact, the only time I have found suitable shoes in those years was in 2004 while holidaying near Geneva, and they were brown unfortunately.

I am afraid to say that my hope remains with you Ms Scott, and I believe that somebody connected with your club may know the whereabouts of my shoe, or saw something that might help us with our inquiries.

Would it be possible to place a small article in your next matchday programme in the hope that it jogs someone's memory? It could read as follows:

'Lost: Black Brogue (Size 10). Were you at Strathclyde Homes Stadium on 23/08/08 for the match with Stenhousemuir? Did you see a lone size 10 black brogue for the left foot? Did you see anything suspicious or unusual that could be connected to this loss? Please contact Rowan Scott at the club if you have any information. Owner desperate to be reunited with shoe. Reward offered.'

I haven't decided on the reward yet but I feel that mention of it may encourage people to come forward. Perhaps your stadium announcer could also read out this piece before the game and then again at half-time for any fans without a matchday programme.

It would mean so much to me if you were able to assist with this and I look forward to hearing your thoughts.

Best Wishes,

Struan J. Marjoribanks

61

19th October 2008

Ms Rowan Scott
Administrator
Dumbarton Football Club
Strathclyde Homes Stadium
Castle Road
Dumbarton, G82 1JJ

Dear Ms Scott,

Have you found it yet?

It is becoming rather embarrassing going to the factory each day wearing one black brogue and one moccasin style slipper.

I simply cannot find shoes to fit you see, and I may need to go down the bespoke road should your news be of a disappointing nature. But I am now prepared for the worst, so go on hit me with it..........

Best Wishes,

Struan J. Marjoribanks

Dear Struan,

You do not know me and I wish to remain anonymous for the moment. I am aware that at a recent visit to Strathclyde Homes Stadium you lost something dear to your heart. I have come into possession of said article.

Your account of losing the item would I feel make an excellent story base for a film. I've thought of a few titles and I am sure the list could go on but I put forward for your consideration,

One Shoe Over The Cuckoo's Nest
Dirty Dancing (one foot only)
Shoeless in Seattle
Footloose
Only Mules and Horses

Perhaps David Sole could play the lead role.

Now lets get down to business. Let me say from the outset that I am not a Dumbarton fan as such however myself and my friends have a loose connection to the club and perform certain duties that others are only to happy to leave to us.

As a small reward to my 6 cohorts I have arranged one of my famous days out on Saturday 8 November. We leave Dumbarton at 10am and travel to Cumbernauld to watch a bowls match. We then intend travelling to Larbert arriving hopefully around 1.30pm where we hope to gain entry to Larbert Bowling Club and indulge in much social drinking prior to the game.

If this plan works out it is within Larbert Bowling Club that the handover of your possession will take place. All you have to do is come to our table and say *"hello boys, I really hope that your team wins today"* and your shoe will be returned. Any deviation from the password will result in you never seeing your shoe again.

You will obviously recognise us as we will be the ones with a shoebox on our table. We will no doubt recognise you as you will be the guy with one shoe. If you fail to attend then I am afraid that your shoe is off to the big cobblers in the sky.

A Friend

9th November 2008

Mr A. Friend
c/o Ms Rowan Scott
Administrator
Dumbarton Football Club
Strathclyde Homes Stadium
Castle Road
Dumbarton, G82 1JJ

Dear Mr Friend,

Many thanks for your anonymous and somewhat mysterious undated letter. My shoe had been found which was wonderful news, but it appeared to be in grave peril, so I did not know whether to laugh or cry. As it happened I did both at the same time, which in weather terms would be represented by the creation of a rainbow.

Unfortunately it was impossible to make the handover meeting at Larbert Bowling Club yesterday at 1.30pm as I only received your letter at 10.49am yesterday. Also, as I'm sure you are aware there was a large inter-county archery competition taking place yesterday afternoon, and my son Daniel (8) was competing as usual. Unfortunately it takes me considerably longer to drive anywhere now that I have only one shoe, which meant there was no way that I could meet with you *and* give my son the attention and support which he requires. However, it turned out that the event was in a rather muddy field which forced me to watch on from the car anyway.

I was, however, delighted to read about your film idea, and I too agree that the plight of a wider-than-normal-footed man who loses a shoe, and then faces a race against time to prevent the dastardly Larbert Bowling Club Gang from condemning him to a life of hopping misery is a splendid idea.

I have noted your title suggestions with interest, and offer the following as potential alternatives should one meet with your approval:

Dr Shoe-vago
Lace Off
My Left Foot (it is the left brogue which went missing after all)
Brogueheart

On the face of it the former Scotland rugby captain David Sole is a fine choice for playing me as he is macho, rugged, and has dark hair. However, given his lack of acting experience I have reservations about his ability to produce a convincing portrayal of the pain and inconvenience which this regrettable episode has caused our soup mogul hero (me).

Your letter ended on a chilling note which sent a shiver down my spine, and albeit apprehensively I must ask if as a result of failing to make the rendezvous my shoe has now gone to the 'big cobblers in the sky'? If so do you have their phone number?

I look forward to hearing from you and hope all is not lost for my brogue.

Best Wishes,

Struan J. Marjoribanks

64

END OF
CORRESPONDENCE

karen hart's factory interview 2008 (unsuccessful)

question 1

i feel quite strongly that carrots are better than onions. you have five minutes to convince me otherwise, starting now

question 2

sing me a song which you feel accurately reflects your desire to work here

question 3

sometimes when sport's on the telly i cry. is teamwork important to you?

question 4

please provide an example of a time when your actions significantly improved the life of a child and/or animal

31st July 2008

Mr Lachlan Cameron
Chairman
Ayr United Football Club
Somerset Park
Tryfield Place
Ayr
KA8 9NB

Dear Mr Cameron,

I had never been to a football match before (it's not really my kind of thing I'm afraid), but I decided to take my son Daniel (8) to your long serving groundsman's recent testimonial match against Rangers Football Club. Daniel is quite a fan of groundsmen and tells me that their good work often goes overlooked, so we went along to offer our support.

I enjoyed the evening but feel duty-bound to inform you that I found the excessive spitting on display utterly abhorrent. The players were at it from the word go, the coaching staff and substitutes were at it, and I believe that both managers could also be seen violently ejecting their phlegm from time to time. As perhaps the only member of the crowd not paying too much attention to the actual play on the pitch I was able to pick up on these things.

I am not wishing to land any individuals in what I would call 'soapy bubble', but I did count your right back spitting eleven times (yes, eleven) in the second half alone! Had it been a spitting match rather than a football match then Ayr United would have won hands down, and would probably be regular winners of the Spitting Champions League I shouldn't wonder.

Upon leaving the ground I asked Daniel if he had enjoyed himself, and indeed he had. I then asked him if he too felt that the inordinate amount of spitting had marred the evening somewhat - he shrugged his shoulders and said that he hadn't noticed a thing. This came as a relief as Daniel can be so easily led, however, upon returning to our car Daniel spat on the windscreen twice. So my point, Mr Cameron, is that the actions of your staff can have a profound influence on impressionable youngsters such as my son.

The following questions need answers before I could return to Somerset Park with my son:

1. Is all of this spitting in football really necessary?
2. Is it simply a result of peer pressure? - 'the left back is doing it and I'm the right back, so I'd better do it too' sort of thing?
3. Most importantly, what can your club do to help stamp out this disgusting habit?

I really do look forward to hearing your thoughts regarding this matter, and hope that Ayr United is able to take the lead on this issue and become the first club to introduce an anti-spitting initiative. I'm sure you will agree that should spitting cease to be a tolerated part of football then the game would be a considerably better, not to mention cleaner, place for it.

Best Wishes,

Struan J. Marjoribanks

66

Ayr United Football & Athletic Club Ltd.

Struan Marjoribanks

██████████████████
████████████
███████

August 11, 2008

Re: Letter dated July 31, 2008

Dear Struan,

Thank you for your letter. I have been on holiday for the last fortnight, so I apologise for the delay in response.

Unfortunately, spitting is part of not only football, but any sport that requires a heavy aerobic output. The athletes struggle to swallow because of the exertion put out and without going into detail, it is easier for them to spit than swallow.

I think you will find that off of the field, they are not inclined to spit in their daily routines, it is purely when they are engaged in sport and on grass.

There is a big difference between spitting during sport and for no reason at all. I understand that it is not pleasant, but it is part of the game. I hope that you show your son this letter and explain to him that it is not socially acceptable to spit on the windscreen nor anywhere else inappropriate, and that these players are not spitting for fun, but rather because they find it difficult to deal with the build up in their mouths.

I realize that this may not be the answer you were looking for, but I hope it helps.

Regards,

Lachlan Cameron
Chairman
Ayr United FC

67

17th August 2008

Mr Lachlan Cameron
Chairman
Ayr United Football Club
Somerset Park, Tryfield Place
Ayr, KA8 9NB

Dear Mr Cameron,

Many thanks for your letter dated 11th August 2008. I trust that you had a pleasant holiday - were you anywhere nice?

I found your letter to be very informative indeed, as not being a particularly sporty gent (don't shoot me!) I have long since forgotten about the advantages of spitting versus swallowing while engaged in a heart-racing physical act.

My son, Daniel (8) was so excited to see a letter from the chairman of a football club that he agreed never to spit in an inappropriate place again. He now fully understands that footballers would not spit on their car, in their kitchen, or at their nanny if they had one (Daniel does, and did, and she was not happy).

Daniel plays for a wee kiddies football team and I went along to watch him on Saturday morning. When the opposition were awarded a penalty the ball was placed on the spot at which point Daniel raced forward and violently 'gobbed' (his description) on it.

Well, as you can imagine I was mortified. The referee brandished a red card immediately and ordered Daniel in no uncertain terms to leave the field of play. Daniel was incensed and trudged off the park shouting: 'What is the problem? Spitting is part of football! My dad's got a letter from a football club which says so.'

It also came to light later that there had been two further unsavoury spitting-related incidents in the game – as Daniel had taken it upon himself to advise his friends that if they want to spit lots then as long as they do it on the football pitch it is acceptable.

I have tried to talk to Daniel about this several times, but he keeps referring to your letter saying that it overrules me as the chairman of a football club understands the game far better than I. Daniel also pointed out that badminton 'requires heavy aerobic output' yet the badminton court at the Olympics is not awash with spittle. I think you will agree that he may have a point there, and that football appears to be unique in this regard.

Would you be willing to assist me in nipping this problem in the proverbial bud? Given the influence your letter has had on Daniel would you be able to write explaining that the football pitch is not a spitting arena per se, and that spitting is tolerated **only** within the professional game (or some other explanation which will bring an end to this sorry episode)?

I hope that you will find it in your heart to help me here, and I very much look forward to hearing from you. Daniel has brought shame on our family through spitting and what we all need now is (as our American cousins might say) closure.

Best Wishes,

Struan J. Marjoribanks

END OF
CORRESPONDENCE

68

Ms Gillian Donaldson
Chief Executive
Greenock Morton Football Club
Cappielow Park
Sinclair Street
Greenock, PA15 2TY

Dear Ms Donaldson,

I was in a real rush to get to Cappielow Park for the match against Dundee on Saturday 25th of October, as not only had I taken my son Daniel (8) to his archery lessons that morning, but when I returned home I received an unscheduled telephone call from Cousin Bryce in Australia updating me on the latest twists in his court case.

By the time I managed to get into my car to drive to the game I was in such a tizzy that I did not notice a hedgehog sitting in the middle of the road and I ran right over it. It was not deliberate, it just happened. I stopped and got out of the car to see if there was anything I could do, but the mess on the road told me otherwise.

I have searched for answers and still I cannot find them. My wife tells me that it is just one of those things, like hayfever, and that I should get on with my life. However, I believe in karma and I therefore believe that bad things may happen to me as a result of taking that hedgehog's life.

One boy that I knew at school took great delight in pulling the wings off of flies, daddy-long-legs, dying bees, dragonflies, moths and any other winged creature that he could get his hands on. He was very badly burnt in a fireworks accident when he was fifteen. What might happen to me?

It was by selfishly rushing to a Morton match that I took that poor hedgehog's life, and I am wondering if the club can assist me in bringing closure to this sorry episode. I feel that any sort of gesture which the club can make to acknowledge my grief and regret would perhaps allow the spirit of that hedgehog to offer me forgiveness and rest in peace.

I understand that a minute's silence at the next home match may be a little excessive, but if the players were able to wear black armbands, for example, or if a message of remembrance could be printed in the matchday programme, then I feel it would help me move on.

The co-operation of the club would be greatly appreciated, as I have bottled this up for the last few weeks and have been unable to attend a match since then as a result.

I look forward to hearing from you.

Best Wishes,

Struan J. Marjoribanks

GREENOCK MORTON FOOTBALL CLUB LTD.

18 74 Cappielow Park, Sinclair Street, Greenock PA15 2TY
Tel: 01475 723571 Fax: 01475 781084 email: info@gmfc.net

3rd December 2008

Mr Struan Marjoribanks

Dear Mr Marjoribanks,

Many thanks for taking the time to write to me regarding the unfortunate event of October 25th which has obviously caused you so much distress.

Having carefully considered the contents of your letter, I can appreciate why you feel that involving our Club may help you to atone for this incident, however can I suggest that there may be a more rewarding way for you to cancel out your actions in the name of Karma than a message of remembrance in our programme?

I'm sure you will be aware of Hessilhead Wildlife Rescue Trust, based in Beith; however you may not be aware that they have a specialised hedgehog unit on site which cares for hedgehogs that are sick or have been injured. As Hessilhead are an independent charity, they rely on funds being raised through membership and their excellent "sponsor-a-patient" scheme as well as other fund raising events.

I have enclosed details of these schemes for your information, as personally I cannot think of a better way to redress the karmic balance than to help other hedgehogs who perhaps find themselves injured as a result of human actions.

I hope that you are able to move on from this incident, and also trust that your Cousin Bryce achieves the desired outcome in his court case.

Yours sincerely

Gillian Donaldson
Chief Executive

70

Directors: DDF Rae (Chairman) • Iain D Brown c.a. • Jim McColl • Arthur Montford • Crawford Rae

Hessilhead Wildlife Rescue Trust

Home	What's On	How to Help	First Aid	Photo Gallery	Gay's Diary

Home
What's On
How to Help
First Aid
Photo Gallery
Gay's Diary
Gifts
Contact Us

Hessilhead cares for Scotland's injured and orphaned wildlife

The centre is situated near Beith in North Ayrshire.

It occupies a 20 acre site, including woodland, marsh and open water. This gives a variety of release sites for our patients.

Facilities at the Centre include an intensive care unit, a swan/seal hospital with indoor pool, a hedgehog unit, a surgery with x-ray equipment and more than 60 outdoor aviaries, enclosures and release pens.

The centre operates a 24 hour emergency service.

Hessilhead is not generally open to the public. This is because our patients are wild, and wild birds and animals are usually frightened of people. Regular disturbance would upset the patients, hamper their recovery, or result in hand reared youngsters becoming tame.

Hessilhead holds one Open Day a year. This is the second Sunday in June, from 12 noon till 4pm. On this day we aim to show the work of the centre, and guided tours round some of the aviaries, enclosures and hospital will allow visitors to see some of the youngsters being hand reared. Please don't ask to be shown round at other

71

Home   Sponsor a Pati   Volunteering

How you can help

Home

Sponsor a Patient

Volunteering

Hessilhead is an independent charity. Funds are raised through the Membership and Sponsor-a-Patient schemes and through fund raising events.

1   MEMBERSHIP   You can support Hessilhead by becoming a member.

Receive two newsletters a year.

Ordinary membership   £12 a year

Family membership   £16 a year

Make regular donations by standing order

Please contact Hessilhead for Membership, Gift Aid and Standing Order forms.

2   Sponsor-a-Patient   see page

3   Volunteer   a   as a daily volunteer (see volunteer page)

               b   as a resident volunteer (see volunteer page)

               c   Help with fund raising. This could be helping with stalls at

72

7th December 2008

Ms Gillian Donaldson
Chief Executive
Greenock Morton Football Club
Cappielow Park
Sinclair Street
Greenock, PA15 2TY

Dear Ms Donaldson,

I am delighted to say that your letter dated 3rd December 2008 has given me a new lease of life, and I really cannot thank you enough! Your incredible foresight and presence of mind has lifted a weight from my shoulders and has shown me the light at the end of this very dark tunnel. For example, just yesterday I drove again for the first time since *the accident*.

I am ashamed to admit that due to work and family commitments the Hessilhead Wildlife Rescue Trust was unknown to me prior to receiving your letter: but what fantastic work the Hessy (as I've taken to calling it) does for wild animals which have suffered a fate not quite as tragic as that of the hedgehog whose life was taken under the wheels of my car.

You may be glad to know that I will be sending a donation to the Hessy to go some way towards atoning for my actions. I feel that £8.00 should be adequate as I would imagine that if hedgehogs were sold as pets they would cost no more than say guinea pigs or hamsters. Don't you think that sounds about right?

Wouldn't it be a lovely Christmas gesture if the playing staff at Morton entered the Hessy's 'sponsor-a-patient' scheme in order to help those less fortunate than themselves? Well, I would like to propose just such an initiative - would you be willing to put that to the players on my behalf? Great positive publicity would obviously be generated for the club, but just think what it would mean to those homesick furry and feathered inmates.

Your kind words regarding Cousin Bryce were also greatly appreciated, although he is what the American might call a 'bad 'un'. If we think of the family in footballing terms then Cousin Bryce would be the goalkeeper who inexplicably allowed a tame back-pass to bobble over his foot and into an apologetically gaping net, or the penalty taker who despite missing five of his last six spot kicks insisted on taking the deciding kick in a penalty shootout only to miss the target completely and require a police escort from the field of play.

Ms Donaldson, I cannot express my gratitude adequately to you for putting me in touch with the Hessy. It was thoughtful, appropriate and inspired in equal measure – *you go girl!*

Finally, I wish yourself and all at the club a very happy and peaceful Christmas, and I look forward to hearing your thoughts on my proposal for a festive Morton-Hessy collaboration.

Best Wishes,

Struan J. Marjoribanks

73

alex ferguson is apparently a **very** capable manager, so much so that i believe his management style is often likened to mine. three people asked me in the same week if it was true that alex ferguson applies an atrological formula to his management in much the same way i do. i did a little research and the result was staggering:

ABERDEEN FC 1986 - ALEX FERGUSON'S ASTROLOGICAL FORMULA

alex ferguson actually uses the exact same astrological formula as me: no geminis in the team (disruptive), and a single mustachioed taurean leader (head chef douglas sinclair in my case)

NORTH OF ENGLAND

- EVERTON
- BRADFORD CITY
- YORK CITY
- MANCHESTER UTD
- PRESTON NORTH END
- BARNSLEY
- LINCOLN CITY
- DONCASTER ROVERS
- MIDDLESBROUGH

struan's north of england facts

the yorkshire moors were a nasty lot in the middle ages; plundering and pillaging wherever they went, before careering down a hill in a bath tub and comically ending up in a duck pond

the scarecrow was invented in sheffield during the industrial revolution

2.5% of men aged over forty in this area have asked that 'fog on the tyne' be played at their funeral

represents the reluctance to acknowledge or react to inclement weather

27th October 2008

Mr Alan Bowen
Head of Stadium Operations
Everton Football Club
Goodison Park
Goodison Road
Liverpool
L4 4EL

Dear Mr Bowen,

My son Daniel (8) has followed Everton ever since my housekeeper Mrs Adams mentioned in passing several years ago that Liverpool FC was evil. Between you and I Mrs Adams can be a daft old bat at times and I therefore paid her no attention, but her remark seemingly made quite an impression on a young Daniel.

Daniel's love of your club has certainly blossomed since then and he has been nagging me for some time to take him to Goodison Park for a match. I finally relented at the beginning of this season and promised that as a birthday treat I would do just that.

Now, I am not a football man Mr Bowen and I am slightly embarrassed to admit that I have never been to a football match in my life. I prefer a good book to be perfectly honest (I'm reading 'Jaws' by Peter Benchley at the moment). You see, as a sufferer of severe tourettes syndrome I try to avoid public outings as much as possible, and although I know that punishing myself in this manner is not the answer I have regrettably allowed myself to become something of a recluse.

I am told that football is more of a family affair than it once was, and I am concerned that 'industrial language' (if I am permitted to call it that) will simply not be tolerated within your stadium. Am I likely to be asked to leave the stadium for the repeated use of obscene language?

It would be a tragedy if we were to travel all the way to Liverpool to watch a game of football only for Daniel's big day to be ruined when his father is ejected from the stadium for inappropriate language after only three or four minutes of the match. Just to give you an idea of the severity of my condition I would estimate that I have sworn loudly around seventeen times in the short space of time it has taken me to write this letter.

As you will understand it would be very beneficial for us to gauge the official Everton policy on profanity inside the stadium before purchasing match tickets and making travel arrangements, and I therefore hope that you are the right person to assist with this query.

I look forward to hearing from you.

Best Wishes,

Struan J. Marjoribanks

76

Mr Struan Marjoribanks

31 October 2008

Dear Struan

Thank you for your letter dated 27 October 2008.

The policy at Everton FC in relation to the use of foul and abusive language is similar to that at all other professional football clubs; it is not tolerated. Under our Ground Regulations my stewards have the authority to eject any person found using such language and indeed the police may arrest such a person.

We would not wish that to happen to anyone like yourself who suffers severe Tourettes syndrome.

We do have an idea as to how we may help you to attend Goodison Park with your son, without suffering the indignity of ejection or arrest. It would assist if you could indicate when you wished to visit us so that we may progress that idea.

Yours sincerely,

Ray Foy
Head of Stadium Safety and Security

77

The Everton Football Club Company Limited
Goodison Park, Liverpool L4 4EL
Registered Number 36624, England

Tel   0870 442 1878
Fax   0151 286 9112
Web evertonfc.com

MAIN PARTNER   OFFICIAL RETAIL PARTN

4th November 2008

Mr Ray Foy
Head of Stadium Safety and Security
Everton Football Club
Goodison Park
Goodison Road
Liverpool
L4 4EL

Dear Mr Foy,

Your letter dated 31st October was very warmly received in the Marjoribanks house let me tell you, and my son Daniel (8) went literally loopy when he saw the official Everton FC headed notepaper. He ran round the living room screaming 'Everton wrote, Everton wrote!' which was a very special moment for all of us.

What was so refreshing about your letter is your ability to see beyond the label of Tourettes and the barrier that it all too often poses. It also sounds like you may be hatching a rather cunning plan regarding our visit to Goodison Park, and despite not wanting you to land in 'scratchy stubble' (trouble) as a result, I would not dream of talking you out of it.

In terms of the match we are wishing to attend, it will not be until the early part of 2009. My wife managed to find a couple of minutes at the surgery yesterday to look at your web, and after consulting one of her male colleagues advised that February looked promising for our visit.

Apparently Everton have home matches against Bolton Wanderers and West Bromwich Albion in February, and although I must confess that I have never heard of these teams Daniel says that they are 'quite rubbishy' (his words, not mine) and hopefully that will allow us to get tickets for either match without too much trouble.

So Mr Foy, please let me know how we proceed from here, and I'd absolutely love to hear what your idea is for bending the rules regarding my foul language. Forgive me, but this is very exciting for me as I have only encountered one other 'official' in recent years who has been willing to bend their rules on obscene language sufficiently in order to grant me access to their venue (in case you are interested that was the concert promoter for Scottish pop band Texas in 2004).

Thanks again for your assistance with this matter. I feel that you have substantially exceeded the call of duty, and from my brief dealings with your club I can see exactly why Everton claim the slightly grandiose title of 'The People's Club.'

I look forward to hearing from you.

Best Wishes,

Struan J. Marjoribanks

END OF CORRESPONDENCE

78

my appearance on 'saturday kitchen' once famous

yorkshire james: i'm yorkshire born and bred unlike our special guest. probably why he's wrote a book of stupid letters to football clubs. proper knob-'ead. why did you bother?

me: (eating a kinder egg) i don't really know

yorkshire james: (shakes head) what's your idea of food heaven?

me: full fry

yorkshire james: (grinning obnoxiously) a yorkshire classic that, lad. and your idea of food hell?

me: full fry without black pudding

yorkshire james: bloomin' nora, what a waste of my very valuable time!

17th September 2008

Mr Jon Pollard
Secretary
Bradford City Football Club
Coral Windows Stadium
Valley Parade
Bradford
West Yorkshire, BD8 7DY

Dear Mr Pollard,

My son Daniel (8) is a keen follower of Bradford City despite our obvious geographical separation, and Daniel tells me that his choice of club was decided in a playground game called 'Club of Life'. Apparently that is generally how these things are decided nowadays.

On Thursday evenings I take Daniel to Mrs Telford's house for piano lessons. Daniel is a promising young pianist, but like most youngsters he would prefer to practise his archery or go hiking in the country rather than practise his scales indoors.

Mrs Telford therefore felt that it might be a good idea for Daniel to learn to play a song dear to his heart to which Daniel immediately suggested your club anthem 'Carpet on His Head'. Daniel informs me that 'Carpet on His Head' is about former player Ben Muirhead's haircut, and although this seems a little silly (if I may be so bold) I am happy to sanction this choice of song if it will encourage Daniel to take his piano lessons more seriously.

Daniel hummed the tune to Mrs Telford and she knew the name of the song that your anthem is based upon. Unfortunately, however, Mrs Telford does not have the sheet music for this song, and neither did our village shop.

I am therefore hoping that you might be in a position to provide the sheet music for 'Carpet on His Head'. I would be very happy to receive a simple photocopy of the music if you are able to provide it, and I would be delighted to reimburse any costs incurred.

Your help with this matter would be greatly appreciated, as I fear this is the last chance for Daniel to find a love for the piano which sadly evaded both his mother and I in our youth.

Best Wishes,

Struan J. Marjoribanks

Bradford City Football Club Ltd

Struan Marjoibanks

22 September 2008

Dear Mr. Marjoribanks,

I am in receipt of your recent letter about our club anthem.

However having made several enquiries nobody has ever heard about any form of song relating to Ben Muirhead.

It is generally recognised that "City till I die" is the Bradford City anthem.

Kind regards,

Yours sincerely,

Jon Pollard
Football Club Secretary

Bradford City Football Club Ltd - Coral Windows Stadium - Valley Parade, Bradford - West Yorkshire BD8 7DY - Tel: 01274 773355 - Fax: 01274 773356
email: bradfordcityfc@compuserve.com - enquiries@the-bantams.co.uk - www.bradfordcityfc.co.uk - bradfordcity.wap.com - Registered No. 05102915 England

Mr Jon Pollard
Secretary
Bradford City Football Club
Coral Windows Stadium
Valley Parade
Bradford, West Yorkshire, BD8 7DY

Dear Mr Pollard,

Thank you so much for your speedy response dated 22nd September 2008 and for endeavouring to answer my query. Your efforts are very much appreciated.

Poor Daniel (8) was so disappointed to read that those within the club were unaware of 'Carpet on His Head' that he cried for over an hour: however, that is a separate discipline issue, the blame for which could never be placed at Bradford City Football Club's door.

Incidentally, 'Carpet on His Head' seems to be a very simple song indeed, and the lyrics are as follows:

> *He's got a carpet on his head,*
> *He's got a carpet on his head,*
> *He's got a carpet on his head,*
> *And his name is Ben Muirhead*

Do you still not know it?

We have actually obtained a copy of the music for this song since I wrote to you, as it turns out that my housekeeper Mrs Adams is very good friends with Mr Fortescue the church organist and he had the sheet music all along.

Daniel has therefore been able to learn to play the song on the piano (it is a simple tune after all) and he has entered his school talent show in which he intends to wear a Bradford City replica shirt on stage and play 'Carpet on His Head' on the piano while his friend Alan Carmichael sings.

I am concerned, however, that as a club you may be unhappy about the promotion of this mystery song. Can you please confirm that Daniel and Alan can enter the competition performing 'Carpet on His Head' with the full blessing of Bradford City Football Club?

As I'm sure you can understand we would hate for Daniel and Alan to do well in the competition only to hear that your club has outlawed 'Carpet on His Head.' Your club's permission to perform this song in public would mean the world to them, and although rehearsals are going well it would help galvanise their focus on delivering the performance of a lifetime.

I look forward to hearing from you, and hope that I will have good news to pass on to the boys.

Best Wishes,

Struan J. Marjoribanks

Bradford City Football Club Ltd

1 October 2008

Dear Mr. Majoribanks,

Further to your letter dated 27 September 2008 I would confirm that we as a club, certainly have no objection to your son performing the song in his school talent show to which we wish him every success.

Kind regards,

Yours sincerely,

Jon Pollard
Football Club Secretary

83

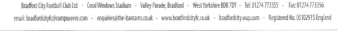
Bradford City Football Club Ltd - Coral Windows Stadium - Valley Parade, Bradford - West Yorkshire BD8 7DY - Tel: 01274 773355 - Fax: 01274 773356

email: bradfordcityfc@compuserve.com - enquiries@the-bantams.co.uk - www.bradfordcityfc.co.uk - bradfordcity.wap.com - Registered No. 05102915 England

8th October 2008

Mr Jon Pollard
Secretary
Bradford City Football Club
Coral Windows Stadium
Valley Parade
Bradford, West Yorkshire, BD8 7DY

Dear Mr Pollard,

Your prompt reply dated 1st October 2008 was most gratefully received. The speed of your response allowed Daniel (8) and Alan (also 8 I think) an extra couple of days rehearsal.

That additional time allowed the boys to nail the song and produce a splendid rendition on Tuesday at the talent show. Alan even managed to remember all of the words, which during rehearsals had been a problem. Without your assistance this may not have been possible.

Our heartfelt thanks go to yourself and to all at Bradford City Football Club for your generosity and understanding with this matter.

On a slightly sour note Daniel and Alan came a lowly fifth in the talent show, but Daniel's mother and I were immensely proud of our son's efforts. Naturally Daniel's disappointment led to many tears (two and a half hours) and even an idle threat to run away from home – but you know what kids are like at that age.

Strangely the school Headmistress Mrs Glanville believed the song to be 'mildly racist'. We were dumbfounded by this accusation and in all honesty are still coming to terms with it. Can something (a song or otherwise) be 'mildly racist?' Moreover, would you describe 'Carpet on His Head' as anything other than good, clean fun?

Mrs Glanville advised that she had guessed that Ben Muirhead was of ethnic origin from the content of the song, and on that basis alone believes the song to be 'mildly racist.' Have you ever heard such incongruous delusional twaddle in all of your life? I suggested to Mrs Glanville that any footballer could have a hairstyle of an equally carpet-like nature, regardless of their ethnic makeup, but by that time she had made up her tiny mind on the matter.

I told Mrs Glanville that I would be asking Mr Muirhead's former employers for their take on the song and that I would get back to her regarding this matter. Are you able to offer your thoughts on 'Carpet on His Head' in order to help settle this debate? For example, have you ever been made aware of a grievance that Ben Muirhead may have had regarding this song?

Your assistance, as always, is greatly appreciated, as this sorry end to what had been a most enjoyable project for Daniel and Alan has left the boys (and myself) more than just 'mildly upset.'

I look forward to hearing from you and thank you in advance for giving up just a little more of your valuable time to my family and I.

Best Wishes,

Struan J. Marjoribanks

84

Bradford City Football Club Ltd

Struan Marjoribanks

9 October 2008

Dear Mr. Marjoribanks,

Further to your recent letter I can only repeat what I have said before, that we have no knowledge of the song.

However what I can say is that Ben Muirhead is not the sort of person to have taken offence at something as trivial as to his hairstyle!

Kind regards,

Yours sincerely,

Jon Pollard
Football Club Secretary

Bradford City Football Club Ltd - Coral Windows Stadium - Valley Parade, Bradford - West Yorkshire BD8 7DY - Tel: 01274 773355 - Fax: 01274 773356
email: bradfordcityfc@compuserve.com - enquiries@the-bantams.co.uk - www.bradfordcityfc.co.uk - bradfordcity.wap.com - Registered No. 05102915 England

Mr Ben Muirhead
Alfreton Town Football Club
The Impact Arena
North Street
Alfreton
Derbyshire, DE55 7FZ

Dear Mr Muirhead,

First of all please accept my humble apologies for contacting you out of the blue like this. I suspect that you appreciate more than most just how rocky the road can be along which we walk on life's great journey. After all Manchester United to Alfreton Town is quite a journey (if I may be so bold), but you have lived the dream and that is more than most of us have ever done.

Jon Pollard at Bradford City advised me that you were not the kind of character to take offence at a song about your haircut – and I am, of course, referring to the Bradford City anthem 'Carpet on His Head.' My son, Daniel (8) performed this song at his school talent show last week sparking a blaze of controversy in the process, and I therefore wonder if you would be kind enough to answer the following questions:

1. Do/Did you find 'Carpet on His Head' offensive?

2. Have you ever suspected the song of being 'mildly racist'? (Mrs Glanville the school headmistress did: the silly old trout).

3. In your opinion can something (a song or otherwise) be 'mildly racist'? (Mrs Glanville obviously thinks it can, but can something as serious and poisonous as racism be 'graded' in the same way as say curry, a cold, or the wind?).

As a family we were flabbergasted at the accusation of Daniel's performance being in any way offensive, and we hope that you will agree with us about the innocent and harmless nature of 'Carpet on His Head.'

I told Mrs Glanville that she had not heard the last from me on this matter, and if the subject of the song agrees that it is no more than good clean fun then she will not have a leg to stand on.

We look forward to hearing from you on this matter and wish you and all at Alfreton Town well.

Best Wishes,

Struan J. Marjoribanks

END OF CORRESPONDENCE

new game proposal: club of life

(to be sent to big games manufacturers such as mb and nintendo)

introduction: dear game manufacturer, i have devised a quite brilliant and inexpensive game called 'club of life' this game is the craze sweeping our country's playgrounds and is now the generally recognised way in which children decide which football team they will support for the rest of their lives. however, nobody has had the foresight to manufacture and sell the components required to play the game......until now!

the game: cut along the perforated lines of the attached club sheet to give sixty (yes sixty!) individual club cards. these are each folded over so that the text cannot be seen and then placed in a hat or a bag. the child requiring a club to support then picks out one of the pieces of paper (much like adults might in an office sweepstake) to reveal the name of the club that they now support.

rrp: 4.99 gbp.

potential customers: parents of children who like football but have not yet succumbed to peer pressure. children who really can't make up their minds about a team and need assistance. adults who have come to football very late (women?).

projected worldwide sales figures: these projected sales figures for the next three years are for worldwide sales and come from extensive recent research:

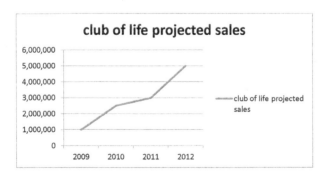

future editions: 1. genus edition (every single british football club)

2. deluxe european edition (features glamour clubs of europe such as barcelona, milans, steau bucharest etc)

3. american sports (features baseball, gridiron, basketball, rugby etc)

stoke city	arbroath	yeovil town	notts county	aberdeen	sheffield united
rochdale	bolton wanderers	charlton athletic	dundee united	chelsea	darlington
albion rovers	watford	liverpool	southampton	wrexham	rangers
blackpool	aston villa	raith rovers	bradford city	chesterfield	newcastle united
wigan athletic	falkirk	preston north end	millwall	arsenal	cowdenbeath
fulham	crewe alexandria	leeds united	manchester city	port vale	montrose
swindon town	everton	oxford united	celtic	bristol rovers	peterborough united
shrewsbury	st johnstone	hartlepool	sunderland	hibernian	leyton orient
tranmere rovers	tottenham hotspur	huddersfield	barnet	cardiff city	hearts
motherwell	swansea city	middlesbrough	crystal palace	leicester city	manchester united

5th September 2008

Mr Nick Bassett
Secretary
York City Football Club
Kit Kat Crescent
York, YO30 7AQ

Dear Mr Bassett,

I think you will agree that several of York City's performances away from home last season were lacklustre to say the least. Indeed, the phrase 'no place like home' could well have been coined with York City in mind - however I (and a couple of others who I have asked) suspect it was coined well before the club's inception in 1922.

'Why do the players seem de-motivated for games away from home?' I asked myself, and the answer came to me in a flash – it must have something to do with the music on the team bus.

Everything on an away trip is out of the club's hands to a certain extent – the length of the journey, the volume of traffic, the conditions in the away dressing room, the number of opposition fans etc. But what *is* in the club's hands is the music on the team bus - and this is where I would like to offer my help.

I've got some real rip-snorting CDs which help motivate me no end. For example, I often listen to the Top Gear Anthems CD when I'm racing to my factory in the morning and trying to beat my time from the previous day. Perhaps the current choice of music on the York City team bus is not energetic and rousing enough to induce this kind of motivation and manic will to succeed.

What I propose to do is to compile a couple of CDs (or tapes if it is an older bus) using the sort of inspirational and explosive rock classics that will get the players fired up for even the unglamorous Non-League games currently being played by the club.

The other thing that I can provide is CDs (or tapes again) of Life Coaching sessions by highly regarded motivational speakers. These won't teach the players how to take a corner kick which beats the first defender, or how to deploy the off-side trap successfully, but they will help the players to discover what they want out of life, and give them the necessary tools to achieve their goals - that to me could only mean 'hello League football' for York City!

Our factory team has been using these motivational tapes for a couple of months now on the mini-bus going to away games and they have been a great success. We beat the McGarvey Bakery team for the first time in our history two weeks ago which just proves how powerful these coaching aids can be.

Please let me know whose attention to mark the CDs (or tapes) for and where to send them (stadium, bus depot, training ground etc). Then we can all look forward to better results away from home this season and hopefully the deluge of silverware that this brings.

Best Wishes,

Struan J. Marjoribanks

89

9th September 2008

Struan J Marjoribanks

Dear Struan

Away Performances

Thank you for your letter dated 5th September in connection with "lacklustre" away performances.

For your information our record last season reads;

Home; Played 23 Won 8 Drawn 5 Lost 10
Away; Played 23 Won 9 Drawn 6 Lost 8

Hardly lacklustre when you're away form is better than your home form!

Thank you for your offer of tapes/CD's; I think we'll decline on this occasion. Perhaps you should research more thoroughly in future!

Yours Sincerely

Nick Bassett
Secretary

90

ork City Football Club Ltd · KitKat Crescent · York · YO30 7AQ
lephone : 0870 7771922 · Fax : 0870 7741993 · Email : info@ycfc.net
atron : The Most Reverend and Right Honourable Dr John Sentamu, Archbishop of York

OUR COMMUNITY FOOTBALL CLUB

gistered in England : 04689338 · VAT Reg No : 809336031

www.ycfc.net

11th September 2008

Mr Nick Bassett
Secretary
York City Football Club
Kit Kat Crescent
York, YO30 7AQ

Dear Mr Bassett,

Heartfelt thanks for your letter (nay lesson in research) dated 9th September 2008. Admittedly my face did redden somewhat as I read your later, but I had hardly made a *faux pas* of Byzantarian proportions!

After all, I saw your team's performances at Broadfield Stadium (Crawley Town) and Aggborough (Kidderminster Harriers) where the demeanour of the York City players was more akin to that of funeral parlour directors than professional footballers.

It saddens me that you do not wish to take up my offer of making specially selected compilations of motivational CDs/tapes (dependent on age of bus): but I respect your opinion in this regard and take it to be the final say on the matter.

However, perhaps the almost unique possession of a better away record than home record requires some further investigation by the club. The following questions are those which immediately spring to my mind, and hopefully they may assist the club in turning round its home (mis)fortunes:

1. Is the ventilation in the home dressing room adequate? Naturally footballer's lungs require substantial oxygen regeneration at half-time and the ventilation in the dressing room is key to this.
2. Is the pre-match diet of the York City player's too rich? The travel involved in matches away from home may make for a lighter and healthier pre-match routine.
3. Do the players bond significantly on the bus going to away matches resulting in a togetherness that is simply not there for home games? Perhaps the players should drive to a designated location some distance from York prior to home games and then be bussed to the stadium together in order to recreate this camaraderie.

Just some ideas for you Mr Bassett, and I look forward to hearing your thoughts on them. I would dearly love to be at least partly responsible for the turnaround in home form which will make York City genuine title contenders this season.

Best Wishes,

[signature]

Struan J. Marjoribanks

END OF CORRESPONDENCE

91

25th March 2012

Manchester United Football Club
Sir Matt Busby Way
Old Trafford
Manchester
M16 0RA

Dear Manchester United,

One of the lads in my soup factory is a very keen astronomer. By day he is a tin-labelling operative, but at night Brian's telescopic lens roams the solar system in the hope of making a celestial discovery (or at least to see something more interesting than what's on the telly – that's just one of my regular little jokes with him).

Unfortunately the other factory workers are a little less tactful and tease Brian mercilessly. They refer to him as 'Telly Scope-Alas', 'Mystic Keg' (we don't actually have soup kegs), 'Jiggy Stardust', 'Buzz Quitequeer' etc etc. Brian is a great lad and outwardly appears to take it all in his stride but it must get to him.

The reason that I am writing to your football club is that Brian hopes that he may have discovered a new star recently and naturally he is over the moon (sorry I couldn't resist another of the little innocent jokes that I share with him). However, being a shy lad Brian wouldn't dream of blowing his own trumpet about the potential discovery.

I asked Brian what he would call the star should it be a new discovery and he told me that he had not given its name any thought. After some gentle probing Brian revealed that he is a massive fan of Manchester United and I suggested that perhaps he could name the star after the football club that he loves so much.

I am therefore writing to you with a general query at this stage. Has your football club ever had a star named after it before? If so what name was used so that Brian avoids duplication, and if not, would your club have any issue with Brian naming the star after your club in some way?

I would like to thank you in advance for your assistance with this matter and Brian and I eagerly await your response.

Best Wishes,

Struan J. Marjoribanks

NO RESPONSE

92

Ms Janet Parr
Club Secretary
Preston North End Football Club
Sir Tom Finney Way
Deepdale
Preston
Lancs, PR1 6RU

Dear Ms Parr,

I hope that you are well and enjoying your position at such a well-loved and historically significant football club. My son Daniel (8) is very keen to try living in England, and as I am nearing retirement age after a very successful career in soup (if I may say so myself) we will soon be able to do as we please.

Preston is one of the places that Daniel has suggested for relocation although I am slightly embarrassed to admit that it is an area that remains relatively unknown to me.

Would you be kind enough to answer the following questions in order to help us choose between Preston and the Cotswolds:

- What is it that you like most about living in the Preston area?
- Are you familiar with the quality of schooling (private) in the area?
- Do the shops in town provide everything required for the 'ladies that lunch' types?
- 3 words if you can to describe the average Prestonian.
- Is the Preston dining experience more 'pie, chips and a pint of bitter,' or '*filet mignon* and a glass of bubbly what'sit'?

I thank you in advance for your help, and I do appreciate that this is a slightly unusual request. However, your famous football club is the first thing which comes to mind when I think of Preston and I simply couldn't think who else to ask.

I look forward to receiving your thoughts, and I wish your club well for the new season. Who knows, perhaps I will soon be cheering the team on in person!

Best Wishes,

Struan J. Marjoribanks

ADDRESS: PNEFC, SIR TOM FINNEY WAY, DEEPDALE, PRESTON, LANCASHIRE, PR1 6RU
TELEPHONE: 0844 856 1964 **TICKET HOTLINE:** 0844 856 1966 **CLUB SHOP:** 0844 856 1965
[CALLS CHARGED AT NATIONAL RATE] **EMAIL:** ENQUIRIES@PNE.COM **FAX:** 01772 693366

PRESTON NORTH END FC

Struan Marjoribanks

2 September 2009

Dear Struan

Thank you for your letter dated 28 August 2009.

I will try and answer your questions as follows:

I have always lived in the surrounding area of Preston so am unable to comment as I have not lived anywhere else to compare to.

I am not familiar with private schooling, although my children attend quality state schools.

Preston is wide ranging you can get pie and chips, Asian, Chinese, Japanese, French etc. and I am unable to comment on whether it is a 'ladies that lunch' type place as it is not something I do.

Thank you for your best wishes.

Yours sincerely

JANET PARR
Secretary

94

nterprise   Club and Shirt Sponsor   WEBSITES: WWW.PNE.COM, WWW.MYPNE.COM
REGISTERED IN ENGLAND NO: 01621060 VAT NO: GB 636 690 121

7th September 2009

Ms Janet Parr
Club Secretary
Preston North End Football Club
Sir Tom Finney Way
Deepdale
Preston
Lancs, PR1 6RU

Dear Ms Parr,

What a thrill it was for Daniel (8) to read your letter dated 2nd September, and I wish to thank you for taking the time to answer my questions. I am delighted to tell you that your charming response has tipped the balance in favour of Preston as far as our relocation is concerned – Daniel just adores Japanese food!

Daniel was so excited by the arrival of your letter that he took it to school today to show his friends. So consumed by jealousy was the class bully, Robert Millard, that he snatched your letter and waddled off with it. Regrettably Daniel never saw the letter again.

Neither Daniel nor I can recall if you said that you were the 'ladies that lunch' type or expressly stated that you were not. If it was the former would you be kind enough to supply a list of the boutiques and eateries frequented by yourself and the girlies in order that I can pass it on to my wife. Alternatively, if it was the latter please accept my sincere apologies.

Either way your response would be ever so gratefully received as Daniel would love the opportunity to take another letter to school from a football club in order to have the last laugh at Robert Millard's expense. I appreciate that seeking revenge is a little immature, but can you just picture Millard's face?!

Many, many thanks for all of your assistance and we look forward to hearing from you.

Best Wishes,

Struan J. Marjoribanks

95

ADDRESS: PNEFC, SIR TOM FINNEY WAY, DEEPDALE, PRESTON, LANCASHIRE, PR1 6RU
TELEPHONE: 0844 856 1964 **TICKET HOTLINE:** 0844 856 1966 **CLUB SHOP:** 0844 856 1965
(CALLS CHARGED AT NATIONAL RATE) **EMAIL:** ENQUIRIES@PNE.COM **FAX:** 01772 693366

PRESTON
NORTH
END
FC

Struan Marjoribanks

2 September 2009

Dear Struan

Thank you for your letter dated 28 August 2009.

I will try and answer your questions as follows:

I have always lived in the surrounding area of Preston so am unable to comment as I have not lived anywhere else to compare to.

I am not familiar with private schooling, although my children attend quality state schools.

Preston is wide ranging you can get pie and chips, Asian, Chinese, Japanese, French etc. and I am unable to comment on whether it is a 'ladies that lunch' type place as it is not something I do.

Thank you for your best wishes.

Yours sincerely

JANET PARR
Secretary

96

11th September 2009

Ms Janet Parr
Club Secretary
Preston North End Football Club
Sir Tom Finney Way
Deepdale
Preston
Lancs, PR1 6RU

Dear Ms Parr,

Thanks ever so much for your lightning quick response dated 2nd September (again!).

It was nothing short of genius to re-send your original letter given the circumstances. Robert Millard's face was out of this world when his beady little eyes saw your identical second letter, and apparently he even did a comedy-like double take such was his disbelief! By all accounts his jaw could have been scraped up off the playground tarmac. *Back of the net!!!*

Fortunately Daniel (8) captured the moment on his mobile telephone's camera (you know what kids are like nowadays), and we have decided to have t-shirts made up with Millard's aghast face emblazoned across the front of them.

It goes without saying that we simply couldn't have done this without you and I am therefore going to have a t-shirt made up for you too. If you could let me know what size you are I would be much obliged, and please also advise if you would prefer the t-shirt to be salmon, charcoal or avocado.

I look forward to receiving your order and thank you once again for not only your quick thinking but also the speed at which you acted upon it.

Best Wishes,

Struan J. Marjoribanks

Struan Majoribanks

24 September 2009

Dear Struan

Thank you for your response and sorry for the delay in replying.

There is really no need to have a t-shirt made up for me, perhaps you could get an extra one for one of Daniels friends. I am sure Daniel would appreciate that more.

Thank you for your best wishes.

Yours sincerely

Jan.do

JANET PARR
Secretary

nterprise
Club and Shirt Sponsor
WEBSITES: WWW.PNE.COM, WWW.MYPNE.COM
REGISTERED IN ENGLAND NO: 01621060 **VAT NO:** GB 636 690 121

my four trips to the barbers in 2010

12th march

barber: do you remember in the
1970s when that guy from
bannockburn took one
hundred penalties for
charity wearing wellies
filled with oxtail soup?

me: no

21st june

barber: see in that world cup
in 1982 – espain '82 –
remember the hondurans
all got food poisoning
from that hot'n'sour soup
in their hotel?

me: no

1st october

barber: i think it was dino zoff
who said that his long
career was down to eating
cabbage and apple soup
twice a day. do you make
that in your factory?

me: no

23rd december

barber: would you invest your
soup wealth in a soccer
school in africa? funny
we'd call that a 'soccer
school' and not a
'football school' eh?

me: no

Mr Barry Taylor
Director
Barnsley Football Club
Oakwell Stadium
Barnsley
South Yorkshire
S71 1ET

Dear Mr Taylor,

My son Daniel (8) has spent the last nine Saturday mornings painstakingly drawing your club crest with an attention to detail that would make some professional artists blush.

We met a lovely family (the Stewarts) while holidaying in Berwickshire earlier this year and they are regular attendees at Oakwell Stadium. Their eldest son, also Daniel, gave my Daniel a Barnsley FC replica shirt to symbolise the friendship that had been forged between our families during those ten special days.

The shirt means so much to Daniel that he often wears it in bed and then to school under his school shirt (despite it being two sizes too big for him), and it is this new-found love of your club that resulted in Daniel embarking on his ambitious drawing project.

Daniel has also asked me if I could commission a life-sized mosaic of your club crest using pieces of coloured glass – each of the men depicted in your crest would be approximately five and a half feet tall.

The Stewarts will be spending New Year with us at our home and ideally I would like to have the mosaic ready in time for their arrival. We all believe that they would be simply thrilled to see not only a beautiful piece of original artwork involving their cherished football team, but also a permanent reminder of the special friendship which our families now share.

I have found a young local artist who is prepared to take on the commission at relatively short notice and they believe that they can have it completed well before Christmas which is splendid news.

Can you please confirm that there are no legal implications that I should be aware of regarding an artist recreating your club crest in such a manner. As you will appreciate it is important to know this before I instruct the artist to commence work. The glass is to be imported from Spain and you could imagine my horror if the order was placed only to find that there is a copyright infringement which prevents the creation of such an *objet d'art*.

I trust that you will be able to assist with this inquiry and I look forward to hearing from you so that we can get the proverbial ball rolling.

Best Wishes,

Struan J. Marjoribanks

BARNSLEY FOOTBALL CLUB

Oakwell Stadium Grove Street Barnsley South Yorkshire S71 1ET

Telephone: 01226 211211 Fax: 01226 211444 Email: thereds@barnsleyfc.co.uk Website: www.barnsleyfc.co.uk

22nd September 2008

Mr. S J Marjoribanks

████████████
████████████
███████
██████

Dear Mr Marjoribanks

We acknowledge receipt of your letter dated 15th September 2008 regarding your intention to commission a mosaic of Barnsley Football Club.

As a Company we have no objection to you re-producing our crest providing it is not for commercial gain.

The commission that you have authorised is quite a task and I would appreciate a photograph once it is complete and we will then make reference to this in our Match Day Programme.

Yours sincerely

A D Rowing
General Manager/Director

101

Barnsley Football Club 2002 Limited
Vat No. 856775960   Registered in England No. 4573250

Mr A D Rowing
General Manager / Director
Barnsley Football Club
Oakwell Stadium
Barnsley
South Yorkshire
S71 1ET

Dear Mr Rowing,

Many thanks for your prompt response dated 22nd September 2008, and for your generous permission to proceed with my mosaic commission. This came as a great relief, and I will be sure to send a photograph of the finished piece – currently scheduled for the second week in December (fingers crossed!).

I have had several meetings with Corben (the artist) since my last letter and they have not passed without incident. Corben knows that I would struggle to find another artist capable of completing the work in this time-scale, and that a better established artist could charge thrice as much as she is charging. As such Corben feels that she is in a position to exercise some artistic license in the piece: albeit this is expressly against my wishes.

There are three things I would therefore like to ask (reluctantly) as a result of our meetings:

1. Could the man on the left of the crest become of ethnic origin to reflect the cultural diversity of modern day Britain and the prominence of non-white footballers throughout the land? This was not my idea naturally, but Corben feels it is important.

2. Could the man on the right of the crest become a woman? This was Corben's idea again (you know what these hippy chicks are like). According to Corben women are making up larger percentages of football crowds each year and that women's football is also becoming extremely popular (is it?), and this mosaic therefore represents an opportunity to recognise women's important contribution to football today.

3. They are out of yellow glass in Spain and it is proving difficult to source here also. This is apparently due to unusually low sulphur supplies. What other colour would be most suitable for the shield on the crest?

I apologise for troubling you with these questions but I have asked Corben to hang fire with her work until we receive confirmation that Barnsley Football Club is comfortable with the alterations proposed.

I look forward to hearing from you and thank you in advance for your assistance, patience and understanding.

Best Wishes,

Struan J. Marjoribanks

BARNSLEY FOOTBALL CLUB

Oakwell Stadium Grove Street Barnsley South Yorkshire S71 1ET

Telephone: 01226 211211 Fax: 01226 211444 Email: thereds@barnsleyfc.co.uk Website: www.barnsleyfc.co.uk

7th October 2008

Mr S J Majoribanks

Dear Mr Majoribanks

We are in receipt of your letter dated 25th September 2008 and have noted your comments in respect of the proposed amendments to the Barnsley Football Club Crest.

As you will appreciate the Coat of Arms is representative of the Barnsley District depicting both a Mineworker and a Glassworker both of whom are an integral part of the Towns' history.

I appreciate that we live in an ever changing society but Corbens' wish to exercise artistic licence may not reflect the views of those families whose ancestors worked in those industries which were the catalyst for the creation of the Barnsley Crest.

I suppose we could liken Corbens' request to asking Everton to substitute a castle on their crest to a bungalow and Tottenham Hotspur replacing their cockerel with a horse.

On a serious note as the Crest is to be given to a Barnsley family it should stay as it is, however I am sure Corben in time will find a way of incorporating her ideas in a future assignment.

Yours sincerely

A D Rowing
General Manager/Director

103

Main Club Sponsor   Official Kit Sponsor   Club Sponsor

Barnsley Football Club 2002 Limited
Vat No. 856775960   Registered in England No. 4573250
For security and training purposes telephone calls may be recorded

11th October 2008

Mr A D Rowing
General Manager / Director
Barnsley Football Club
Oakwell Stadium
Barnsley
South Yorkshire
S71 1ET

Dear Mr Rowing,

Thank you so much for your letter dated 7th October 2008, it was most gratefully received. I must admit that I did rather chuckle at your analogy regarding Tottenham Hotspur *'replacing their cockerel with a horse.'* Given their abysmal current form perhaps a donkey would be more appropriate!

As for the serious matter of my mosaic commission, I fully understand Barnsley Football Club's insistence that the crest remains as is, and you are preaching to the converted in this regard. I, on the other hand, upon visiting Corben's workshop yesterday was preaching to the perverted.

Corben has quite a mouth on her let me tell you, and after reading your letter she started screaming wildly about 'artistic oppression' and 'female persecution.' I'm sure you've come across these lily-livered arty types before – all nose studs, purple dreadlocks and Socialist Worker subscriptions.

She then said that if the club was bothered about the heritage of the town then why not make both men in the crest at least twenty stone in weight and clutching bags of chips, as apparently Barnsley is in the top ten fattest places in Britain. This seemed like a very silly thing for Corben to say at the time: however two of the Stewarts (our Barnsley friends) are considerably overweight. Do the seats at Oakwell Stadium need to be wider and stronger than standard stadium seats to allow for your disproportionately overweight support?

At that point, as luck would have it, Corben's mobile phone rang and it was her boyfriend Jez saying that the biodynamic farm at which he had been working had gone into receivership. As a result my commission instantly took on greater financial importance to Corben and she sheepishly apologised for her behaviour and admitted that the customer is always right.

So, Mr Rowing, it is full steam ahead with the mosaic at Corben's workshop and I have her assurance that it will be completed as accurately as possible. This only leaves the unanswered question regarding what colour of glass should replace the yellow on the shield. As mentioned in my previous correspondence yellow is unavailable. Would you, as a club, prefer the shield to be completed in flesh or orange coloured glass? These seem to be the best alternatives that our glass supplier can provide.

Your assistance, as always, is very much appreciated, and I look forward to hearing from you in order that we can confirm our finalised order with our Spanish supplier.

Best Wishes,

104

Struan J. Marjoribanks

BARNSLEY FOOTBALL CLUB

Oakwell Stadium Grove Street Barnsley South Yorkshire S71 1ET

Telephone: 01226 211211 Fax: 01226 211444 Email: thereds@barnsleyfc.co.uk Website: www.barnsleyfc.co.uk

20th October 2008

Mr S J Marjoribanks

Dear Mr Marjoribanks

Please forgive me I should have confirmed in my last letter that the colour of the glass to be used in the production of the Crest should be flesh rather than orange.

I have thought long and hard about Corben's comments and under normal circumstances would have let it pass, particularly as I abhor left wing activists. However, in this instance I am going to make an exception.

What I find interesting about people of Corben's ilk is that they are so full of venom and hatred to those with differing views that they lose their sense of reality.

Perhaps, Corben should also consider thinking before commenting on women's oppression, does she not realise that many of the laws passed over the past 30 years have been in the interests of women, passed by the majority of men who I might add have also contributed heavily through taxation to educating her and given her the opportunity of living in her insane dreamland of make believe.

Finally I do wish you every success with the Crest and trust that Corben does not use artistic licence and put "chips" on the shoulders of those representing the working class.

Yours sincerely

A D Rowing
General Manager/Director

105

Main Club Sponsor

Official Kit Sponsor

Club Sponsor

Barnsley Football Club 2002 Limited
Vat No. 866775960   Registered in England No. 4573250
For security and training purposes telephone calls may be recor

24th October 2008

Mr A D Rowing
General Manager / Director
Barnsley Football Club
Oakwell Stadium
Barnsley
South Yorkshire
S71 1ET

Dear Mr Rowing,

If you have ever watched a live golf event from America you will have heard pumped-up and boozed-up frat boy Yanks inappropriately bellowing 'YOU THE MAN!' at the top of the golfer's backswing. Well, Mr Rowing, I am not ashamed to admit that those words involuntarily left my lips as I read your wonderful letter (nay rant) dated 20th October.

I agreed wholeheartedly with every word of your letter, and it is as refreshing as a cold pint of lager shandy on a warm summer's day to hear an official speaking frankly and openly without cow-towing to those PC lefties who have this country in wrack and ruin.

Again I brayed like a foal at your facetious suggestion that Corben may place chips on the shoulders of those depicted in the crest: a beautifully orchestrated *coup de grâce* given Corben's unprovoked attack on Barnsley's fatties and the role chips play in their diet.

Have you ever considered a career in politics Mr Rowing? I suspect that you would enjoy a groundswell of support from the good people of Barnsley due to your forthright and honest opinions, not to mention your quickness of wit and sharpness of tongue.

Many thanks also for confirming that flesh coloured glass would be best for the shield. This was gratefully received and duly noted.

Avoiding any further disputes the mosaic will hopefully be finished on time, and I will be sure to keep you updated on our progress. Also, no need to worry, I will not be allowing Corben to read your most recent letter (it would no doubt be the proverbial straw that broke the camel's back for the ugly man-hater).

Many thanks for all of your help, and in the meantime, up the Tykes!

Best Wishes,

Struan J. Marjoribanks

106

15th December 2008

Mr A D Rowing
General Manager / Director
Barnsley Football Club
Oakwell Stadium
Barnsley
South Yorkshire
S71 1ET

Dear Mr Rowing,

I hope that you are keeping well and that your team are performing as you would wish. I have been informed that the festive period is a busy and vital one in the football calendar, and I therefore hope that when Father Christmas visits Oakwell Stadium his sack is positively groaning with points for Barnsley Football Club.

It pains me to tell you that it looks like being a rather bleak Christmas in the Marjoribanks household, and I am unfortunately writing to you in a state of overwhelming incredulity.

As you will remember I had commissioned a young upstart of an artist by the name of Corben to produce a stained glass mosaic of the Barnsley Football Club crest. Well, I dropped by Corben's workshop yesterday for our usual catch-up regarding her progress with the mosaic as it was due to be completed by Christmas, and when I got there the door was locked with the following hand-written note stuck to the door:

Workshop Closed

Corben and Jez have left The System behind to try life on an Israeli kibbutz, but should be back next year some time. Sorry if your work was not finished in the agreed time, but please take a look around before you point the finger at us. He who points the finger of blame must also blame the finger that points.

Merry Christmas.
Corben

I was utterly speechless. I still am. Fortunately I am still able to type. Needless to say the mosaic will not now be ready for the Stewart family's visit in just a few weeks. I felt I should let you know as you have been so kind over the last few months, and I had promised you a photograph of the mosaic on completion.

I do not mind admitting that I have found my dealings with Corben to be completely baffling. For example, do you know what 'System' Corben refers to, and have you ever heard that guff before about the 'finger of blame'? Absolute drivel if you don't mind me saying so.

So Mr Rowing, I can only wish you, your family, and all at Barnsley Football Club a very Merry Christmas, and I hope that the festive season brings you all the luck and joy to make up for my misfortune.

Best Wishes,

Struan J. Marjoribanks

107

BARNSLEY FOOTBALL CLUB

Oakwell Stadium Grove Street Barnsley South Yorkshire S71 1ET

Telephone: 01226 211211 **Fax:** 01226 211444 **Email:** thereds@barnsleyfc.co.uk **Website:** www.barnsleyfc.co.uk

30th December 2008

Mr S Marjoribanks

Dear Mr Marjoribanks

I trust that both yourself and your family had a good Christmas and New Year and your experiences of 2009 will not include the Anarcho-Libertarian Socialist Corben.

I have thought long and hard about the "finger of blame" and must assume that due to Corben's inability to finish the project (for whatever reason) her only get out is to blame a third party for her inadequacies.

Leaving the system behind I find easier to understand perhaps the cynic in me has helped with this. The system they refer to is of course the Benefit System and I would suspect that neither Corben nor Jez have worked long enough to qualify for the free handouts, and the realisation of having to look for a real job would have made their decision to leave an easy one.

The decision to live life on an Israeli Kibbutz is ok if you wish to live in a commune, personally I would be guided by the guy who said "never go to a place that sounds like a medical condition" and Kibbutz does sound like an incurable disease.

Although our correspondence has covered a number of months I would welcome a letter should our mutual friend feel the need to embrace "the system".

Yours sincerely

A D Rowing
General Manager/Director

END OF CORRESPONDENCE

108

all professional footballers like bon bons. but what
colour of bon bon does the 1986 hibernian squad
like best? you need speculate no further, for here
are the answers:

HIBERNIAN FC 1986 - FAVOURITE COLOUR OF BON BONS?

a quick tally shows pink to be the most popular
which is absolutely mental when you
consider that yellow is the best

Mr Rob Noble
Marketing Assistant
Lincoln City Football Club
Sincil Bank Stadium
Lincoln, LN5 8LD

Dear Mr Noble,

I have only ever met one man without a hobby and that was my Uncle Norris – needless to say that he died a lonely old man, albeit a relatively wealthy one. Most hobbies cost money, but as comedy writing is my hobby it brings in a few pennies here and there.

As a lover of football I am currently writing a comedy sketch regarding the classified football results, and I am hoping to be able to write a sketch with your club's blessing which uses Lincoln City's name in the punchline (but don't worry your club is not the butt of the joke!).

In the sketch there is a middle aged man wearing a sheepskin coat and a flat cap sitting in a small featureless room wearing headphones and reading out the football results into a microphone. The man has horrendously bad wind so after he reads out each away team's name there will be a loud 'farting' noise which corresponds with their score.

So the sketch will work as follows (just to give you an idea):

'Barnet - nil. Chester City, (pause, loud 'farting' noise), one.
Gillingham - three. Bradford City (pause, two loud 'farting' noises), two.'

The man will read through the whole of the division's results in this way until he reaches the final result at which point he defecates himself. The punchline will therefore be as follows:

'Rochdale - one. Linc (pause, loud 'farting' noise) Oln (pause, loud 'farting' noise). Ci (pause, loud 'farting' noise). Ty (pause, very long, wet and loud 'farting' noise). Oh dear, I've shat myself. Four.'

Please excuse the colourful language, but it is required for comic effect I think you will agree. Before I complete the sketch and write it out in the standard script format I just want to check that your club has no objections to being associated with somebody pooping themselves.

If you could please confirm this it would be greatly appreciated, however, I will understand if you are unhappy about your club's good name being used in this way and I can then approach another club. I would hate for the sketch to make it onto television or radio only to upset anyone at your club who feels they should have been consulted first.

I look forward to hearing your thoughts, and hope that as a club you are able to enter into the spirit of the thing and permit me to complete the sketch as intended.

Best Wishes,

Struan J. Marjoribanks

110

LINCOLN CITY FOOTBALL CLUB

SINCIL BANK STADIUM, LINCOLN LN5 8LD

Main Switchboard : 0870 899 2005
Fax : 01522 880020
Website : www.redimps.com
E-mail : lcfc@redimps.com
Stadium Website: www.sincilbank.com

With Compliments

Main Sponsor

Struan,   12ᵗʰ Jan 2009

Happy for you to use our club name in the punchline.

Regards

Rob Noble

ROB NOBLE - MARKETING ASSISTANT

111

18th January 2009

Mr Rob Noble
Marketing Assistant
Lincoln City Football Club
Sincil Bank Stadium
Lincoln, LN5 8LD

Dear Mr Noble,

Thanks heaps for your compliment slip dated 12th January 2009 permitting me to complete my sketch as intended. Your prompt response was very much appreciated.

Since my letter to you the creative juices have been flowing somewhat, and I have had the idea of writing a number of other sketches in a similar vein -- all involving people soiling themselves at the mere mention of Lincoln City. Here are a couple of examples:

Example One - *two middle aged women sitting in a café drinking coffee. Woman One asks Woman Two how her son James is doing in his fledgling football career. Woman Two beams proudly and says that James has been handed a trial at Lincoln City, at which point she lets out an almighty, long, wet 'farting' noise and all of the other customers turn round in disgust and stare at her. Once the noise subsides Woman Two sheepishly says 'sorry everyone, I've just shat myself.'*

Example Two – *a teacher is standing at a blackboard speaking to her class of young children. The letter 'L' is written on the blackboard. She says 'now class, you've all given me lots of words beginning with the letter L. Here's one for the boys. Can anyone tell me the name of a football club beginning with the letter L?' A boy shouts out 'Liverpool.' Another boy, after a few seconds pause, shouts out 'Leeds United.' Then there is silence. 'OK then,' the teacher says, 'what about Lincoln City?'*

Immediately the teacher's face looks concerned and she appears to be in considerable discomfort. Then a long, loud, almost volcanic rumble erupts from her bowels. We see some close-ups of the bemused children's faces, and the noise continues apace as we see more aghast children's faces. Then when the noise eventually stops we see the teacher bent double, holding onto her desk and gasping for air. 'Children,' she says, 'I've just shat myself.'

So what do you think? I feel that the joke is improved considerably through repetition, and what could well happen is that the punchline of 'Lincoln City. I've just shat myself' could become a famous enough catchphrase to have school children repeating it gleefully in the playground at break time (just like 'compootah say no').

Naturally I would not continue with the moulding of this new catchphrase if as a club Lincoln City was unhappy with it. However, as a marketing person you hopefully subscribe to the view that there is no such thing as bad publicity.

I look forward to hearing your thoughts on all this, and many thanks again for your assistance with this matter.

Best Wishes,

112

Struan J. Marjoribanks

Mr Rob Noble
Marketing Assistant
Lincoln City Football Club
Sincil Bank Stadium
Lincoln, LN5 8LD

Dear Mr Noble,

Only me. You will remember that I recently got back in touch with you regarding the proposed comedy catchphrase of 'Lincoln City. I've just shat myself'. I have yet to hear back from you on that, but having given the idea further thought I felt that I must make contact again.

I was in the supermarket this morning and just as I was considering the 'cost versus conscience' debate surrounding battery farm eggs another example sketch using the catchphrase leapt into my mind from nowhere – and it is perhaps the finest yet.

In this latest example we see pictures of an astronaut walking on the moon. We then hear the astronaut's conversation with NASA (Houston, Texas) which sounds the way astronauts speaking to Houston always seems to sound. It would therefore be as follows:

Astronaut: *(American accent) This is a momentous occasion. I may be one of just few, but I represent so many.*

Houston: *(More American accent) Congratulations Jim, we are all so proud of you. Go ahead if you want to take the time to thank some people.*

Astronaut: *Thank you Houston. To my wife, Hayley, and my beautiful children Regan, Chelsea and Kimberline: I love y'all so much, and daddy will be home real soon. (Becoming emotional) To mom and dad: I wish y'all could see me now, and perhaps up here I'm that little bit closer to you. To NASA: great job guys. And finally, to my little brother Aaron who is over in England trying to become a professional soccer player: I did it bro! Now you go and win that contract at Lincoln City.*

(Pause, and then very long, wet 'farting' noise and the astronaut lets out some groans of discomfort as the noise continues. The noise eventually stops and there is a long pause).

Astronaut: *Houston, I've just shat myself.*

I hope you will agree that it was worth me getting back to you on this. I really can envisage great things for this catchphrase, and if picked up by one of the popular sketch shows it could also help raise the profile of your club immensely. I would imagine that shirt sales, for example, would rocket (no pun intended!).

I am very keen to hear the club's thoughts regarding the catchphrase as it is not my intention to upset anyone, and I could substitute the name Lincoln City if required. However, if given the green light then I will be able to write the remaining sketches required, and submit them to the relevant production companies. I therefore eagerly await further instruction.

Best Wishes,

Struan J. Marjoribanks

113

9th April 2009

Mr John Vickers
Media Manager
Lincoln City Football Club
Sincil Bank Stadium
Lincoln, LN5 8LD

Dear Mr Vickers,

As you will be aware I have been in communication with your assistant Rob Noble regarding the new comedy catchphrase *'Lincoln City - I've just shat myself'*.

Mr Noble was kind enough to permit me to use the name of Lincoln City in a comedy sketch which I wrote (I felt it was only right to ask for permission) – and I have no doubts that he will have run that decision by you first.

My last couple of letters to Mr Noble have gone unanswered, however, which is why I am now writing to you. I am hoping to obtain permission from your club to write not just one comedy sketch using the phrase, but a series of sketches. There is absolutely no doubt that such a series of sketches could turn *'Lincoln City - I've just shat myself'* into <u>the</u> latest big comedy catchphrase to sweep our country's playgrounds.

The final sketch in the series (just finished this morning) is set at heaven's gate, so if you can picture two men standing on what appear to be clouds and behind them there is a large shut pearly gate (white?). The man standing in front of the gate is Saint Peter and he is dressed in white robes with a long white beard, while the other man is very normal looking (scruffy even).

Saint Peter: *(Speaking the way we'd expect God to) So, you're brown bread then Simon?*

Man: *(Sad) Yes. Heart attack. How do you know my name?*

Saint Peter: *(Winks) I know everything Simon. Tell me, have you been good down there?*

Man: *(Thinks for a second) I think so. I was only ever in trouble with the law once, and that was years ago when I was arrested for being drunk and disorderly at a football match....*

Saint Peter: *(Interrupting) Yes, I remember it well, it was at Lincoln City.*

Saint Peter immediately begins breathing very heavily and looks to be in serious discomfort. We hear a long rumbling noise followed by an enormous explosion like a volcanic eruption.

Saint Peter: *(After noise eventually subsides. Shocked) Blooming Nora, I've just shat myself.*

What do you think Mr Vickers? Do I have your club's permission to submit the series of sketches to the relevant production companies and broadcasters?

Given the work that has gone into the writing I'm sure that you will understand how much I would appreciate your thoughts on this, and I look forward to hearing from you.

Best Wishes,

Struan J. Marjoribanks

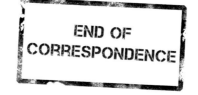

114

15th September 2008

Mr David Morris
Secretary
Doncaster Rovers Football Club
Keepmoat Stadium
Stadium Way
Lakeside
Doncaster, DN4 5JW

Dear Mr Morris,

I have visited Keepmoat Stadium seven times now, and do you know that Doncaster Rovers have won 3-0 each time. Is that some kind of a record, or have you heard of that before?

I have a good friend who is a Cambridge United fan and he has only seen them win 3-0 twice.

My wife had a very quick look at your internet while on her lunch break at the surgery but could see no mention of a club historian whom I could have directed this letter to *à propos* this record.

If you could let me know just how special that record of mine is I would greatly appreciate it.

Best Wishes,

Struan J. Marjoribanks

DONCASTER ROVERS FOOTBALL CLUB

Keepmoat Stadium, Stadium Way, Doncaster DN4 5JW

Telephone: 01302 764 664 Fax: 01302 363 525 Email: info@doncasterroversfc.co.uk

www.doncasterroversfc.co.uk

Mr. S. Marjoribanks

29 September 2008

Dear Mr. Marjoribanks,

Thank-you for your letter referring to your visits to the Keepmoat Stadium, and the co-incidental fact that on each of your seven visits the Rovers have won 3-0 each time. Without consulting the records, I was not aware that we had seven home victories of a 3-0 scoreline during our short time here at the Keepmoat.

The club does have an un-official historian, but I can't see how he can identify whether or not your achievement is a record in comparison to anyone else. However, if you would like to address any correspondence to him, his name is Tony Bluff, and can be contacted by letter through the club's address.

We could do with you coming more often and being our lucky talisman – a few 3-0 victories would be very welcome right now.

Best wishes to you and your family.

Yours sincerely,

Charles Swallow
Customer Services Manager

116

Patienceform Ltd trading as Doncaster Rovers Football Club   Company Reg No: 3739676

Mr Tony Bluff
Unofficial Club Historian
Doncaster Rovers Football Club
Keepmoat Stadium
Stadium Way
Lakeside, Doncaster, DN4 5JW

Dear Mr Bluff,

I received a most heart-warming letter from your leader Mr Charles Swallow dated 29th September 2008. I had written to the club advising that on each of my seven visits to watch Doncaster Rovers they have won 3-0, and I wonder if this is a record.

Mr Swallow suggested that in your capacity as unofficial club historian you would be able to advise if this is a record, or if you have heard of that before.

For your interest the seven visits were as follows:

1. September 16th 1994 versus Hereford: *Invited to the game by well known Rovers fan Russell Campbell. As you'll remember Russell sadly passed away just three months later.*

2. October 19th 1996 versus Brighton and Hove Albion: *Can't actually recall the circumstances.*

3. March 25th 1997 versus Rochdale: *Cousin Bryce was home from Oz and we decided to go along to watch a match.*

4. January 20th 2001 versus Forest Green Rovers: *In the area on business.*

5. December 26th 2004 versus MK Dons: *Another happy Christmas spent at Auntie Jessie's.*

6. January 1st 2007 versus Huddersfield: *More family festive fun at Auntie Jessie's.*

7. April 21st 2007 versus Brentford: *Cousin Bryce's once-a-decade return from Oz and we decided to go along to watch a match.*

Ironically I was due to attend the game on 18th of February 1995 in which Rovers beat Lincoln City 3-0, however the night before the match I slipped and fell in the bathroom after cutting myself quite badly while shaving and I sustained a rather nasty gash to my forehead which unfortunately prevented me from attending.

So Mr Bluff, in your opinion just how special is that record of mine? I am apprehensive about attending another game at Keepmoat Stadium for fear of this remarkable run coming to an end and your assistance would therefore be greatly appreciated.

I look forward to hearing from you.

Best Wishes,

Struan J. Marjoribanks

Mr Charles Swallow
Customer Services Manager
Doncaster Rovers Football Club
Keepmoat Stadium
Stadium Way
Lakeside
Doncaster, DN4 5JW

Dear Mr Swallow,

Please do not think that it is my intention to 'dob in' Tony Bluff, however, after supplying Mr Bluff with the details of my remarkable record I have yet to receive a response from him.

It has become very important to my family and I that we establish just how special my record is. My Cambridge-United-supporting friend (Brian Askew) believes that my record may not just be unique to Doncaster Rovers, but also to British football, and perhaps even Northern European football.

My son Daniel (8) is so disappointed each day when our mail arrives and there is nothing from Mr Bluff that he often refuses to finish his breakfast, and on one recent occasion cried all the way to school, embarrassingly kicking a neighbour's dog *en route*. If you could therefore find the time to follow this up with Mr Bluff I would be extremely grateful.

We greatly look forward to hearing from Mr Bluff (after you have given him a gentle prod), and thank you in advance for your assistance with this matter.

Best Wishes,

Struan J. Marjoribanks

TONY BLUFF
MEDIA DEPT
DONCASTER ROVERS
4.11.08.

Dear Sir,

      I was given a letter dated 25.10.08 on Saturday in which my name is mentioned in regard to writing a letter. There is a perfectly good reason why I hadn't written to you — I was not aware of the need to write!!! I had not been told of your query & knew nothing of it until being handed the above letter.

      Even now I am not too sure that I have been told the exact nature of your query but it would seem that you have visited the Keepmoat Stadium & seen the Rovers win 3-0 on 3 or 7 occasions that you have attended. It can't be 7 because the Rovers have not won 3-0 at the Keepmoat on 7 occasions.

119

So, it must be 3. But how does one quantify such a record? Short of launching a nationwide search among football fans, possibly through the media i.e. newspapers, radio & television, then one cannot know if any of the spectators at a game have a similar record.

Therefore, all I can say is come to the Keepmoat again & let us win 3-0, it is badly needed at this time but unfortunately it is likely that you would spoil your record because we don't have a goalscorer to score the goals!

So, by all means, claim your record until someone else does.

Yours in sport

Tony Bluff.

Mr Tony Bluff
Media Department
Doncaster Rovers Football Club
Keepmoat Stadium
Stadium Way
Lakeside, Doncaster, DN4 5JW

Dear Mr Bluff,

It was with great pleasure that my family and I read your beautifully hand-scribed letter dated 4th November 2008. I was, however, distressed to hear that you did not receive my letter dated 4th October 2008, and therefore apologise for my follow-up letter dated 25th October 2008 which (knowing what I know now) may have been a little heavy-handed. I sincerely hope that my last letter did not land you in 'Barney Rubble' (trouble).

We are in total agreement that it is difficult to quantify this kind of record, but if other fans care not to record the results of matches which they attend then that would potentially be their loss and my gain.

We rejoiced upon reading that you are happy for me to claim my record as Doncaster Rovers' Luckiest Fan. Daniel's (8) face lit up and he did three cartwheels in our living room before collapsing in a fit of the giggles, such was his delight at the news. We then enjoyed a slap up family meal at our favourite local eatery by way of celebration, with Daniel enjoying fish for the first time which was a remarkable and unexpected bonus. And it was all thanks to you!

Would you be willing to put me forward to the Rovers board for the official title of Doncaster Rovers' Luckiest Fan? This would naturally mean the world to myself and my family, and Cousin Bryce has already intimated that he and his family would make the trip from Australia should there be an official award ceremony of some kind. Auntie Jessie (90) would also be proud as punch, and we would do our best to wheel her along too.

If you could let me know what your thoughts are on this it would be greatly appreciated.

On a slightly unhappier note, I was saddened to read that the Rovers are bereft of a goal scorer at present. Chin up Mr Bluff, goalscoring heros often appear from nowhere, and I am confirdent that Rovers will sniff one out sooner rather than later.

I look forward to hearing from you, and many thanks again for the accolade – you really did make my year!

Best Wishes,

Struan J. Marjoribanks

END OF
CORRESPONDENCE

121

my appearance on 'dragons' den' once famous

leatherface dunc: (glowering) i'm probably out and you've not
                     opened your gub yet. why should i even give
                     you the time of day?

me: (smiling in fear) you're welcome. i'm here to
                     tell you about the 'soup pie' which will
                     change the face of catering at football.
                     everyone loves a pie and everyone loves soup.
                     combine the two and you have the 'soup pie.'
                     a traditional pie crust with soup poured
                     securely into it. the delicious warm soup is
                     spooned out in the normal way and then the
                     pie crust can be eaten like a pastry dessert.

leatherface dunc: (impatiently) aye, but is it going to sell
                     millions and make me even more obnoxious?

me: (before leaving in tears) i really don't know

Ms Karen Nelson
Club Secretary
Middlesbrough Football Club
Riverside Stadium
Middlesbrough, TS3 6RS

Dear Ms Nelson,

I hope that this correspondence finds you well. I am an avid collector of many things – from toasters to stamps, and even amphibian taxidermy. I began my most recent collection around six years ago, and it is a collection of the headed notepaper of the professional football clubs of the world.

It is my rather ambitious aim to collect the headed notepaper of every professional football club in the world, and I have been working hard over the last six years to put a dent in this goal. I am very proud to say that I now have 321 items in my collection, and I am hoping that with your assistance that total will rise to 322.

It goes without saying that my goal cannot be achieved without the co-operation of the clubs, and I would therefore be ever so grateful if you were able to furnish me with a letter on Middlesbrough Football Club's headed notepaper.

I have set myself the realistic target of reaching the magical number of 500 letters by the end of 2009.

I very much look forward to hearing from you, and hope that Middlesbrough Football Club will become the latest addition to this fascinating, colourful and unique collection. Also, if you happen to have any old and non-confidential letters from other clubs which you no longer require then I would be absolutely delighted to take them off your hands.

Many thanks in advance for your assistance with this request, and may I also take this opportunity to wish yourself and all at Middlesbrough Football Club a happy and peaceful Christmas and New Year.

Best Wishes,

Struan J. Marjoribanks

Middlesbrough Football Club

Training Headquarters

Rockliffe Park, Hurworth Place, Nr Darlington, DL2 2DU
Tel: (01325) 722222 Fax: (01325) 722104

9th December 2008

Mr. S. Marjoribanks

██████████
████
██████
████

Dear Mr. Marjoribanks

Further to your letter of 30th November, please find enclosed a sample of our letterhead for your collection.

Regards.

Yours sincerely

Karen

Karen Nelson (Mrs)
Secretary

124

● ● ● RACIAL EQUALITY STANDARD
● ● ● PRELIMINARY LEVEL
● ● ● AWARDED BY KICK IT OUT

Riverside Stadium, Middlesbrough, TS3 6RS Tel: 0844 499 6789
Fax: 01642 757697 E-mail: enquiries@mfc.co.uk Website: mfc.co.uk
Middlesbrough Football & Athletic Company (1986) Ltd. Registered in England No.1947851 Vat No. 746 7738 83

Middlesbrough Football Club

Training Headquarters

Rockliffe Park, Hurworth Place, Nr Darlington, DL2 2DU
Tel: (01325) 722222 Fax: (01325) 722104

SAMPLE LETTERHEAD

PROVIDED BY MIDDLESBROUGH FOOTBALL CLUB

AS A COLLECTORS ITEM

NOT TO BE USED UNDER AND CIRCUMSTANCES

125

RACIAL EQUALITY STANDARD
PRELIMINARY LEVEL
AWARDED BY KICK IT OUT

Riverside Stadium, Middlesbrough, TS3 6RS Tel: 0844 499 6789
Fax: 01642 757697 E-mail: enquiries@mfc.co.uk Website: mfc.co.uk
Middlesbrough Football & Athletic Company (1986) Ltd. Registered in England No.1947851 Vat No. 746 7738 63

GARMIN
SAT-NAV

11 December 2008

Mrs Karen Nelson
Club Secretary
Middlesbrough Football Club
Training Headquarters
Rockliffe Park
Hurworth Place
Nr Darlington, DL2 2DU

Dear Mrs Nelson,

Many thanks for your letter(s) dated 9th December 2008. I cannot thank you enough for taking the time to assist what you may have considered to be a 'silly little man with a silly little collection' – but it means a great deal to me as I'm sure you will understand.

I mentioned in my previous letter that if you were kind enough to contribute to my collection that Middlesbrough would be the 322nd club in my collection, but I am delighted to say that the God of Letters has unabashedly spoiled me since I wrote to you, and in that time I have received headed notepaper from Fluminese (Brazil), VfL Bochum (Germany) and Wrexham (Wales). Middlesbrough therefore take the 325th spot in my collection, so congratulations!

It may not surprise you that I keep detailed statistics of my collection, and you may be interested to learn that Middlesbrough is the 19th club crest in my collection depicting a lion (the second most popular animal only to the eagle), and of those club crests displaying the year in which the club was founded Middlesbrough is the 9th oldest club.

There really was no need to send me a second piece of the same headed paper, but it was very gratefully received all the same. My rival Oliver Struver from Salzburg, Austria is working on a similar collection (rumoured to currently have around 200 letters) and this second piece could perhaps be used in a swap for one of his 'doublers'.

Struver recently boasted on an internet forum that he has now 'completed' the Columbian league, and as I have yet to try Columbia then perhaps a trade could be arranged with him. However, I first wanted to check with you that you were comfortable with me swapping the second item of headed notepaper should such an opportunity arise.

I also wanted to ask (and I appreciate that this is a little underhanded of me) that if an Oliver Struver writes to you with a similar request for headed notepaper that you do not respond to him. It is well known that Struver targets female office bearers at football clubs whenever possible as he feels that they are more likely to respond to him, so it is quite possible that when he turns his attention to Middlesbrough Football Club that yours will be the name he plumps for. Naturally I am keen to beat him to the magical 500 letters and I am therefore hoping that you will agree to assist me.

Thanks again for taking the time to contribute to my collection and I look forward to hearing your thoughts *vis-à-vis* Oliver Struver.

Best Wishes,

Struan J. Marjoribanks

126

Middlesbrough Football Club

Training Headquarters

Rockliffe Park, Hurworth Place, Nr Darlington, DL2 2DU
Tel: (01325) 722222 Fax: (01325) 722104

Our Ref KN/KB/01757

16 December 2008

Struan J Marjoribanks

Dear Struan

I refer to your letter of 11 December 2008.

I have no objection to you swapping the extra piece of letterhead paper with your 'rival'.

Furthermore, I will attempt to avoid sending a piece of letterhead to him, however, should one of my colleagues here receive his request that may be difficult.

Once again, thank you for contacting me and best of luck with your collection.

Kind regards.

Yours sincerely

KAREN NELSON
Club Secretary

127

RACIAL EQUALITY STANDARD
PRELIMINARY LEVEL
AWARDED BY KICK IT OUT

Riverside Stadium, Middlesbrough, TS3 6RS Tel: 0844 499 6789
Fax: 01642 757697 E-mail: enquiries@mfc.co.uk Website: mfc.co.uk
Middlesbrough Football & Athletic Company (1986) Ltd. Registered in England No.1947851 Vat No. 746 7738 83

6th January 2009

Mrs Karen Nelson
Club Secretary
Middlesbrough Football Club
Training Headquarters
Rockliffe Park
Hurworth Place
Nr Darlington, DL2 2DU

Dear Mrs Nelson,

Happy New Year to you and all at the club!

It gives me no pleasure to report that an extremely modest Yuletide was had in the Marjoribanks household due to a significant chunk of my life savings being spent on stamps within the last year or so. But please don't fret - we did manage to have turkey on Christmas day, albeit a turkey stir fry using the meat from those excellent value turkey thighs.

My son Daniel (8) had asked for a PS3 (whatever that is) and did grumble a little at the video recorder which I bought him instead, while my wife had to make do with what I had billed as 'a new kitchen', but was actually a set of pots and pans that had been purchased in the January sales a couple of years earlier and then stored away in the loft. Out of sight out of mind. I received stamps from both - so I was well chuffed on Christmas day!

How was your Christmas and New Year?

The only reason I am contacting you again is to thank you for rebuffing the efforts of Oliver Struver when he attempted to obtain a piece of Middlesbrough FC headed paper recently. My mole in the Struver camp has advised me that having written to your club a number of weeks ago Struver has yet to receive a response, and I can only assume that the request came to you as predicted and that you sneakily binned it when nobody was looking.

Are you able to confirm that you thwarted Struver's advances? If so I can then play my trump card which is the offer to swap Struver my Middlesbrough FC 'doubler' for one of his prize Columbian pieces.

You have helped to put me in a very strong position in the race to 500 and I therefore felt that it was only right to express my gratitude in writing (hence the use of yet another stamp).

All the best for 2009 and it would be lovely to hear from you.

Best Wishes,

END OF CORRESPONDENCE

Struan J. Marjoribanks

128

AUSTRIA

home of my rival
oliver strüver!

+─+ LIDL
+─+ MAYOR OF IPSWICH
+─+ MAYOR OF LLANIDLOES
+─+ SCOTTISH RUGBY UNION

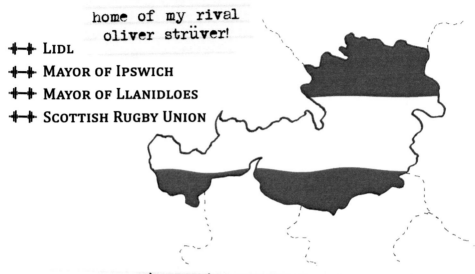

struan's austria facts

+─+ austria is very rarely in the news - even in austria itself - and as a result the national news is often replaced by a rerun of 'entertainment tonight'

+─+ many austrians claim that fencing (the boundary structure - not the sport) began in austria, however, many greeks have vociferously disputed this claim

+─+ the tap water in austria is so cold, clear, and refreshing that fizzy drinks are rare and are therefore prohibitively expensive as a result. a can of fizzy pop currently costs the equivalent of one of those indian style takeaway bags (poppadoms, pakora, onion bhaji, pilau rice, chicken tikka, chicken jalfrezi, small nan bread) in any large british supermarket

+─+ represents what can be achieved if your name is arnold schwarzenegger

Head Office
Lidl
19 Worple Road
London
SW19 4JS

Dear Lidl,

Being that I derive from Austria I am very fan of Geröstete Leber (calf's liver under butter). My biggest upset in UK is that I have none of Geröstete Leber. Lidl is big company near Austria and can bring in Geröstete Leber to UK. Would you possible do this and I buy many pieces?

I am waiting your answer and hope to hear good news. Also, your interest to know I have three friends in UK also deriving from Austria who want Geröstete Leber and buy this too.

Many thanks for any assistance for me.

Best Wishes,

O.R. St

Oliver R. Strüver

Without Prejudice

Mr Oliver Struver

Lidl UK GmbH
Tailend Farm
Deans Road
Livingston
EH54 8SE

Tel: 0870 4441234
Fax: 01506 591540

27 January 2012

Our Ref: 954413 PR 12

Dear Mr Struver

Re: Gerostete Leber – Calf's Liver under Butter

Thank you for taking the time to provide us with your valuable feedback from your letter dated 19th January 2012, regarding the above-mentioned product.

We thank you for your comments, as it is always gratifying to hear that our customers enjoy our products. However we do not stock these particular items in the UK and have different procurement sources to Lidl in Austria.

We will keep your comments onboard for future reference and have informed our Buyers of your request. May we thank you for bringing this brand to our attention and trust that you will continue to be a valued Lidl customer.

Yours sincerely,
For and on behalf of Lidl UK GmbH

Pam Waite
Customer Services

131

Registered office: Lidl UK GmbH 19 Worple Road London SW19 4JS, Registered in England No FC017929, Vat No. GB 614798608

Pam Waite
Customer Services
Lidl
Tailend Farm
Deans Road
Livingston
EH54 8SE

Dear Mrs Waite,

I am thanking you very much for the letter of 27th January that I receive from you today. To receive this quick letter was a very happy thing for me.

Funny story: in this letter you say that I enjoy Lidl products. If I write this then I understand this, but I did not communicate this to you. Is true I enjoy some Lidl products – the Mars bars that are not real are magical value! But the Iron Brew is not enjoyed. No, no, no.

It is very nice of you to tell Buyers of need for Geröstete Leber. Can you now say when they will Buy Geröstete Leber and if I can collect at nearest Lidl to my home or will Geröstete Leber come direct to my home?

I thank you very much for helping with this hunt.

Best Wishes,

Oliver R. Strüver

132

Without Prejudice

Mr Oliver Struver

Lidl UK GmbH
Tailend Farm
Deans Road
Livingston
EH54 8SE

Tel: 0870 4441234
Fax: 01506 591540

08 February 2012

Our Ref: 954413 PR 12

Dear Mr Struver

Re: Gerostete Leber – Calf's Liver under Butter

We refer to your most recent letter dated 1st Febuary 2012, regarding the above-mentioned product.

As previously advised, we do not stock these particular items in the UK and we have informed our Buyers of your request. Unfortunately we cannot advise if this item will be made available in our stores.

With regards to your request for home delivery, unfortunately it is with much regret to advise that at this current stage, we do not have an ordering or delivery service system available. The only way in which to shop with Lidl is by visiting our Stores directly.

Nonetheless, please be advised that we have noted your comments with our Sales Department, as we welcome all feedback from our customers.

In closing, may we thank you for taking the time to contact our Department and trust that you will continue to remain a valued customer of Lidl.

Yours sincerely,
For and on behalf of Lidl UK GmbH

Karyn Meek
Customer Services

133

Registered office: Lidl UK GmbH 19 Worple Road London SW19 4JS, Registered in England No FC017929, Vat No. GB 614798608

14th January 2012

The Mayor of Ipswich
The Mayor's Office
Ipswich Borough Council
Grafton House
15-17 Russell Road
Ipswich IP1 2DE

Dear Mayor of Ipswich John Le Grys,

I hope that I address you correct and sorry if not. I visit Ipswich two times to visit friend Robert (Bob) Turner: great big man with beard and Ipswich Town tattoo on his leg, but I know you will not know him. I very much enjoyed your town.

I am in United Kingdom to complete Honours degree in Abstract Algebra. Funny story: I have already said to run my uncle's pig farm in North West Bavaria! The course is very good fun so I complete before pigs.

I derive from Salzburg, Austria, and we have mayors there. Funny story: in Germany mayors are called *Burgermeisters*, I just now wonder if they are covered in salad and sauce. Or a bun. Or cheese.

Since child I always have interest in mayors and wanted to be mayor for many years. I am enthusiastic art hobby and would like to make your portrait. Could you please send me a photograph of you that I can use for portrait. I would be very thankful if you could as I do portrait of two mayors before now and just now I try to make three.

I thank you and look forward to photograph.

Best Wishes,

Oliver R. Strüver

The Mayor's Office
Grafton House, 15-17 Russell Road, Ipswich IP1 2DE
Telephone: (01473) 432641
Facsimile: (01473) 432033
email: mayor@ipswich.gov.uk

24 January 2012

Dear Mr Struver,

Thank you for your letter of 14th January 2012 to the Mayor of Ipswich, and thank you for your kind comments about our town.

Details about the Mayors of Ipswich, the history and their pictures are available on the Ipswich Borough Council website: www.ipswich.gov.uk/mayors .

There are many pictures of our current Mayor, Cllr John Le Grys on the site, including pictures of some of the civic events that have taken place in Ipswich during his year in Office.

I hope you find this information useful, and we wish you well for your future studies.

Yours sincerely,

Christine Christensen (Mrs)
Civic Secretary – Mayor's Office

Mr Oliver R Struver
██████████████
████████
███

135

28th January 2012

Mrs Christine Christensen
Civic Secretary
The Mayor's Office
Grafton House
15-17 Russell Road
Ipswich IP1 2DE

Dear Mrs Christensen,

I am thanking you very much for your letter of 24th January. This came very well received and so excited to receive this letter was I that I turn on my computer to go straight to the website of Mayor John Le Grys that you told me of. Wow, I could not believe how much Mayor John Le Grys is looking like my friend Bob Turner! Funny story: I have to take two looks to be sure he is not Bob!

So I make portrait of the first photograph I find of Mayor John Le Grys as I like it very much. A man of power, a man of statute in society and photograph shows him drinking beer with great smile on his face. This photo allows me to see the real man of Mayor John Le Grys.

I wanted Mayor John Le Grys to have this portrait that I make. I hope that he enjoys this portrait and believes I made good portrait of him. Finally, I thank you once more for telling me where to go for this picture I can use.

Best Wishes,

Oliver R. Strüver

mayor of ipswich john le grys

O.R.St.

mayor of ipswich at beer festival

Mayor John Whittal Williams
Llanidloes Town Council
Town Hall
Great Oak Street
Llanidloes
Powys
SY18 6BN

Dear Mayor John Whittal Williams,

Your town became aware to me in 2005 when I was playing a man called John from your town in game of online chess. Since I have visited your town on three times and it is my hope to visit again before it is my time to return to Austria.

Today I read Cambrian News (online version) and was sad to read of problems with rats and doggy messes in your town. This story from your town made me think of my similar story from Berchtesgaden which is town near Salzburg. There some many years ago there was a problem with rats. A group of vicious dogs was breeded to remove rats from that town. Over two week time scale people of Berchtesgaden had what I think translate as 'curfew' at 8pm and hunger dogs let out of cages then. Dogs find rats and eat them and then gathered by special men and returned to cages in morning by 7am when people of Berchtesgaden allowed to leave homes again.

After two weeks of this work with vicious dogs not a rat seen again in Berchtesgaden. Of course the problem of doggy messes was increased, but we have a saying in my part of Austria which translate I think as 'one backward step to be alright if forward steps is two.'

Perhaps in your town you can do same method as Berchtesgaden so to remove rats first and then take steps after this for clean of doggy messes. Looking forward for hearing your thoughts to this proposal and it is my hope that it fixes your town's need.

Best Wishes,

Oliver R. Strüver

NO RESPONSE

138

7th February 2012

Scottish Rugby Union
Murrayfield Stadium
Murrayfield
Edinburgh
Midlothian
EH12 5PJ

Dear Scottish Rugby Union,

Being that I am from Austria (Salzburg) your sport of rugby was not known to me
when I reach UK for doing Honours degree in Abstract Algebra. This sport has been
fascinated by me since when I have been here. In Austria it is not possible to see
anything like this anywhere! Funny story: not even in the night after pubs close!

When this degree is finished it will be that I need to return to Austria. Have you
known of rugby anywhere in Austria? If this is so then can you tell me to where I
must go. If this is not so, how would it be possible to bring this wonderful sport to
Austria? This I think could be my life's work.

I look forward to receiving your thought on this and I thank you very much for
introduction to the best sport to see.

Best Wishes,

Oliver R. Strüver

139

Ref: KEM/charities
Io 9 February 2012

Oliver R Struver

Scottish Rugby Union plc
Murrayfield
Edinburgh EH12 5PJ
T: 0131 346 5000
F: 0131 346 5001
www.scottishrugby.org

Dear Oliver

Rugby in Austria

Thanks very much for taking the time to write on 7 February 2012 to inform of your great enjoyment of our Great Game of rugby, which has recently been introduced to you here in Scotland.

There is indeed the Austrian Rugby Union ("**Rugby Austria**"), and the contact details for this Union are as follows:

> **Address**
> Schönbrunnerschloss strasse 52
> Vienna
> 1130 Austria
>
> T: +43 664 7355 8864
> E: a.langerhansel.rugby@aon.at
> www.rugby-austria.at

According to their website, which I have accessed through the **International Rugby Board's** website, their **Chairman** is **Alexandra Langer-Hansel**, and the Union's **President** is **Andreas Schwab.** I do not know if these details are still the same - you may wish to access their website for more information.

I am enclosing a double-sided mini poster of the Scotland National Squad 2011/12 on the one side, and on the reverse the Scotland Women Squad 2011/12. I also thought you might enjoy receiving the latest edition of our own publication *TeamTalk* which has lots of interesting rugby news and goings on, here in Scotland.

140

Once again, thanks very much for writing, and I do sincerely hope that you will now be able to follow Austrian rugby, as well as, of course, take part in many of the Scottish rugby matches which will be taking place all over Scotland - as well as those further afield throughout the UK - for the remainder of Season 2011/12.

You may wish to access the **Glasgow Warriors Club's** website, too, which is more your side of the world (Renfrewshire), but at any rate you will have much to absorb through a visit to our own website - www.scottishrugby.org

With best wishes to you

Kathleen Munroe
Kathleen Munroe
Governance Administrator
Legal & Governance Support Department

T: 0131 346 5102 (direct)
E: kathleen.munroe@sru.org.uk

enclosures: 2

141

SCOTLAND SQUAD 2011-12

Back row: Scott Lawson, Euan Murray, Nikki Walker, Scott MacLeod, Jim Hamilton, Richie Gray, Sean Lamont, Graeme Morrison, Moray Low, Joe Ansbro
Middle row: Ben Cairns, Dougie Hall, Alex Grove, Greig Laidlaw, Jim Thompson, Alasdair Dickinson, Richie Vernon,
Kelly Brown, Rory Lamont, Max Evans, Ruaridh Jackson, Ross Rennie, Rory Lawson, Alan MacDonald, Geoff Cross
Front row: Allan Jacobsen, Gregor Townsend *(Scotland coach)*, Dan Parks, Nathan Hines, Andy Robinson *(Scotland head coach)*,
Mike Blair, Chris Paterson, John Barclay, Hugo Southwell, Graham Steadman *(Scotland coach)*, Ross Ford

Follow Scotland on twitter @Scotlandteam

SCOTLAND WOMEN SQUAD 2011-12

Back row: Sarah Dixon *(Stirling County)*, Megan Gaffney *(Murrayfield Wanderers)*, Katherine Muir *(Richmond)*, Anna Swan *(RHC)*, Jemma Forsyth *(Hillhead /Jordanhill)*, Lana Skeldon *(Melrose)*
Middle row: Andrew Easson *(assistant coach)*, Karen Findlay *(head coach)*, Ruth Slaven *(Murrayfield Wanderers)*, Tracy Balmer *(Worcester)*, Charlotte Veale *(London Wasps)*,
Lindsey Smith *(Hillhead/Jordanhill)*, Caroline Collie *(OA Saints)*, Suzanne Mckerlie-Hex *(Murrayfield Wanderers)*, Beth Dickens *(Murrayfield Wanderers)*,
Alison Macdonald *(RHC)*, Charlotte Lewis *(Richmond)*, Chris Reid *(assistant coach)*
Front row: Lisa Martin *(Murrayfield Wanderers)*, Katy Green *(Murrayfield Wanderers)*, Stephanie Johnston *(RHC)*, Laura Steven *(Murrayfield Wanderers)*, Lindsay Wheeler *(Darlington Mowden*
Sharks), Susie Brown *(Richmond)*, Louise Dalgliesh *(RHC)*, Heather Lockhart *(Hillhead/Jordanhill)*, Sarah Quick *(Murrayfield Wanderers)*, Lauren Harris *(Melrose)*.

Scotland Women v England Women
Sunday 5 February, 5pm
Lasswade, Edinburgh

FREE ENTRY!

Scotland Women v France Women
Saturday 25 February, 2pm
Bridgehaugh, Stirling

16th February 2012

Kathleen Munroe
Governance Administrator
Scottish Rugby Union
Murrayfield Stadium
Murrayfield, Edinburgh
Midlothian, EH12 5PJ

Dear Ms Munroe,

My thanks for you cannot be enough after receiving your letter and gifts dated on the 10th February. It is my apology for taking so long to reply but as you will know I have much coursework for the degree in Abstract Algebra. If I do not lock myself into the study room I will literally be going crazy trying to watch rugby or learn more of this great game! For that reason I did not open your package before this day.

My eyes did not believe what I was reading and I was not like tough rugby men because tears came close to my eyes. Andreas Schwab is president of Rugby Austria! If this is the same Andreas Schwab this man I knew when I was child because he was shopping regular in my uncle shop for pets in Salzburg. I help there many times and he was buying many mouses for eating of his snakes. In Austria we call this what I think translates as 'how could you ever know such a thing father?' In this country I am thinking this is called an 'amazing coincidence' or some such thing.

Then I look with great interest at the picture of Scottish woman rugby team. I could not believe that women are playing rugby in Scotland. Forgive me but this game is new to me and this I did not know. This game is brutal force and also dangerous! Funny story: these women are not looking like Arnold Schwarzenegger or Claus von Apswolf! They are what you would be calling here 'bonnie lasses.' So I must ask if they play rugby in the same way as men or is there no touching or some such thing in rugby for women?

I thank you very much again for helping me and for gifting me a magazine and team poster. This was extremely kind gesture and has given me unbelievable experience!

Best Wishes,

Oliver R. Strüver

143

the four stages of man (as charted through soup)

the pre-fire age

pre-historic man: i'm back. o.k. -
i've filled the stone pot with bones,
leaves, roots and water. have you
invented the hotty-hotty?

pre-historic woman: no

the age of medicine

sobbing mother: so it is death
plague, doctor. is there anything
at all that we can do for him?

doctor: you still have two options
- brain leeches or chicken soup

sobbing mother: i'll stoke the
fire and butcher gertrude

the industrial age

industrialist: (to large crowd of
workers) work-life balance? well,
we're introducing a 'bring your
child to work' scheme. in return for
their twelve hour shift in the
factory you will get a bowl of soup
if it's a girl, and a bowl of soup
and a slice of bread if it's a boy

the age of celebrity

celebrity chef: (to camera) like
you didn't know already, i'm zander
'soup-maker-to-the-stars' aragones.
my latest invention is soupas -
tapas size capsules of soup. short
bursts of flavour full of soupy
goodness. wedding outfit to get
into? - asparagus and guava. car
to be serviced by that dishy
mechanic? - celeriac and yam.
life's just a breeze with soupas!

WALES

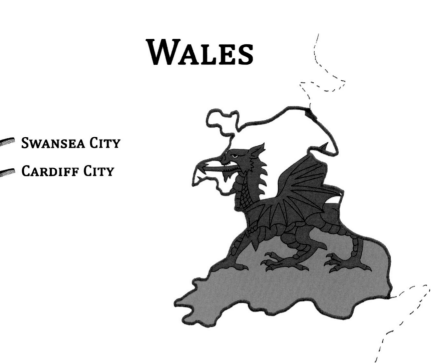

- SWANSEA CITY
- CARDIFF CITY

struan's wales facts

it would take fifty-six million 400g cans
of soup to turn the valleys into soup lakes

footage remains of only five of the seven known
episodes of 'songs of praise' to have been filmed
outside of wales

at any given time between 11am and 11.30pm
(monday to friday) there are around 65,000
welshmen playing snooker

represents the exceptionally
well-turned-out male choirs thereof

24th August 2009

Mr Alun Cowie
General Manager
Swansea City AFC
Liberty Stadium
Landore
Swansea, SA1 2FA

Dear Mr Cowie,

Swansea City has been my team for many, many years. My late grandfather claimed to have shared breakfast with the great Swansea inside-forward Ivor Allchurch in a Cornish hotel during the 1950s. Grandpa's stories of Allchurch's impeccable manners when asking for the marmalade to be passed, and his genuine interest in Grandpa's line of work as a salt merchant made quite an impression on him, and Swansea was adopted as the Marjoribanks' team from then on.

My factory football team has what I would consider to be a disproportionate number of bald players – six of the usual starting eleven. When I joked with one of the players about this he said that baldness often indicated superior co-ordination and that it could be considered an advantage for footballers. Personally I believe this to be nothing more than baldy delusions of grandeur.

Keeping up on all things Swansea it appears to me that there are no bald players within the Swansea City first team squad at present. Shaved heads do not count of course. Are you able to confirm that this is the case? If so are you able to advise me of any standout Swansea players from yesteryear that were naturally bald?

I am pleased to say that It is all in good fun, but there is a small wager riding on this as I advised our factory team that the best team in the land (Swansea City of course!) were baldless, and the lads said that if I am wrong then my forfeit is to play in goals for an entire training session wearing a pair of Sammy McIntyre's pants on my head. If you knew Sammy you would understand the gravity of what is at stake.

Finally, I am currently compiling a list of famous bald footballers for the benefit of my team and I don't mind telling you that I am struggling. So far I have got Bobby Charlton, Attilio Lombardo, Thomas Gravesen, John Hartson, and that guy who played for Southampton in the 1980s whose head was like a little upturned egg. As a football man would you be able to add any names to this list?

I wish you and everyone at your club all the very best for this season, and I will be watching out for your scores with everything crossed each Saturday as I have done for many years. I know that you are a very busy man, but if you are able to assist me with my questions I would be ever so grateful, and I (and my team) look forward to hearing from you.

Best Wishes,

Struan J. Marjoribanks

NO RESPONSE

146

30th October 2008

Mr Ian Lanning
Kit Manager
Cardiff City Football Club
Ninian Park
Sloper Road
Cardiff, CF11 8SX

Dear Mr Lanning,

My son Daniel (8) is extremely keen on football, so much so, in fact, that he has begun spitting and swearing excessively. Daniel's mother and I have now learned that this is just part of football and have come to accept it: although it has caused considerable embarrassment in church as I'm sure you can imagine.

Daniel is a sensible lad and already understands that he does not possess the ability to make it in the game as a professional footballer. However, his love for the game is such that he is already thinking about alternative ways in which he could make a living from football when he is older.

Together we have gone through the many different positions held within a football club to see which Daniel would be best suited to, and I am delighted to tell you that we are in complete agreement that the position of kit man would be Daniel's ideal job. Daniel is personable, good with numbers and quite likes ironing (even at his tender age). The question now is how can Daniel make his dream a reality?

If you could take the time to answer the following questions we would be extremely grateful:

1. Is there any specific advice you could offer Daniel to help him achieve his goal of becoming a kit man?

2. How did you get your big break? Was it the usual 'right place, right time' sort of thing, or did you make up your mind from an early age that you wanted to be a kit man and then banged on the door relentlessly until an opportunity presented itself?

3. What does a 'normal' day consist of for a kit man?

4. Is there an association of kit men which Daniel and I could contact in order to get him on a kit man waiting list if such a thing exists?

I realise that I have asked a lot there, but I have promised Daniel that I will do everything I can to help him land his dream job. I have done some research and you seem to be one of the kit men held in the highest regard within the game, and we would therefore greatly appreciate any help or guidance that you are able to provide.

I look forward to hearing from you.

Best Wishes,

Struan J. Marjoribanks

147

everyone is aware that the 1986 dundee united squad
were a group of extravagant impulse buyers. training
ground bust-ups fuelled by jealousy and consumer
envy were commonplace. you want to know what their
most extravagant impulse buys were, don't you?
i called in a few favours and found out for you:

DUNDEE UTD FC 1986 - MOST EXTRAVAGANT IMPULSE BUYS

snakeskin belt and shoes — JIM McLEAN (MANAGER)

his and hers jetskis — HAMISH McALPINE

full suit of armour — RICHARD GOUGH

glass blowing furnace — PAUL HEGARTY

broken jukebox — MAURICE MALPAS

70% stake in race horse — DAVID NAREY

walk in humidor kit — EAMONN BANNON

timeshare (tenerife) — STUART BEEDIE

three alsations — JOHN HOLT

majolica monkey jug — BILLY KIRKWOOD

stuffed sparrow-hawk — THOMAS COYNE

tanning salon — DAVID DODDS

authentic bobba fet costume — RALPH MILNE

19th century carriage — PAUL STURROCK

East of Scotland

- HEARTS
- LIVINGSTON
- DUNDEE
- ELGIN CITY
- STENHOUSEMUIR

struan's east of scotland facts

- the bermuda triangle was once thought to exist directly above linlithgow

- this is the only area of great britain where cats (domestic, feral and wild combined) are known to outnumber humans

- there is a one mile stretch of coast right up near the top which has been unseen by the human eye for over two years due to relentless and impenetrably high winds

- represents a propensity for moustache growth and cultivation rarely found outside of india or parts of south america

9th October 2008

Ms Julija Goncaruk
Non-Executive Director
Heart of Midlothian Football Club
Tynecastle Stadium
McLeod Street
Edinburgh, EH11 2NL

Dear Ms Goncaruk,

Auntie Jessie has recently turned 90 God bless her soul. This is a remarkable achievement when one considers that she was the youngest of thirteen (yes thirteen!) born in an Edinburgh tenement in the early twentieth century.

Auntie Jessie's husband Archibald died many years ago, but he was a big fan of the Hearts. You know how it was in those days: Archibald would go off to the match with his friends and come home at eleven o'clock at night with a belly-full of ale and a child-making glint in his eye.

When Archibald returned home he would tell Auntie Jessie about the match at Tynecastle in great detail, and then from what I can gather they would make a child. Well, there was no television in those days of course.

As Auntie Jessie gets older her short-term memory is certainly waning, but her long-term memory is quite remarkable. Jessie tells a story about a game Archibald attended in the late 1930s at Tynecastle in which he claims that as the teams emerged for the second half the Hearts goalkeeper strolled onto the pitch eating a bag of chips!

This story has been re-told many times by Auntie Jessie (usually at family functions) and she often re-enacts the scene by trudging round her living room stuffing mints into her mouth and shrugging her shoulders almost apologetically. It is a very funny sight indeed, and a firm favourite with all our large family.

I am keen to discover the truth behind this story, and that is why I am writing to you. Our family is quite literally Hearts daft, and we have always wondered if there was a chip-eating goalkeeper who turned out for Hearts during the war, or if this is just another example of Auntie Jessie's muddled state of mind.

Would it be possible to receive a photograph of the goalkeeper if such a thing exists? I believe this would make dear old Auntie Jessie very happy indeed, and in a sense would bring her dearly beloved Archibald closer to her until they finally meet again.

Auntie Jessie does not know that I have written to the club regarding the goalkeeper, and it will be a lovely surprise for her if you are able to provide information and/or a photograph of this mystery goalkeeper who Jessie holds so dear to her heart.

I hope that you are able to assist with this query and I very much look forward to hearing from you.

Best Wishes,

Struan J. Marjoribanks

150

HEART OF MIDLOTHIAN PLC
TYNECASTLE STADIUM
GORGIE ROAD
EDINBURGH EH11 2NL
T +44 (0) 870 787 1874
F +44 (0) 131 200 7222
www.heartsfc.co.uk

24 October 2008.

Mr.S.Marjoribanks.

Dear Mr.Marjoribanks,

Your letter of 9 October was passed to me on Wednesday for action.

It is a very interesting story but I cannot confirm that it actually happened. I took the opportunity to ask my Archives Group members and one or two supporters who are into everything 'Hearts', again no one had heard the story. All we could come up with was that our goalkeeper at that time – Willie Waugh – was considered a bit of a rebel.

Sadly I am unable to help you give your aunt a pleasant surprise.

Regards,

Alex.H.Knight.
Club Archivist.

22 October 2008.   **151**

REGISTERED IN SCOTLAND No: SC5863

Mr Alex H. Knight
Club Archivist
Heart of Midlothian Football Club
Tynecastle Stadium
McLeod Street
Edinburgh, EH11 2NL

Dear Mr Knight,

Many thanks for your letter dated 24th October and for following up with your Archives Group members and some of the diehard Hearties (would you call them that?) regarding the chip-eating goalkeeper. I really do appreciate your assistance with this matter.

I visited Auntie Jessie on Saturday to break the news to her that I was trying to trace the mystery goalkeeper and to read her your letter. This gave me the opportunity to put the name of Willie Waugh to her to see if it rang any bells.

At the mere mention of the chip-eating goalkeeper we were treated to the customary mint-stuffing routine, and I'm glad to say that it was just as hilarious as ever. Then I mentioned Waugh's name and Jessie's face lit up – it was quite a picture I can tell you. Some 90 year olds rarely smile and when they do it has the ability to melt your heart.

Alas, Jessie was unable to confirm if Waugh was the name associated with the chip-eating episode, but the name triggered another memory of a story told to her by her late husband Archibald. Sometimes the long-term memory of the old and infirm can be quite staggering.

Apparently Hearts were playing at Tynecastle against one of the less fashionable clubs of the time, and were being surprisingly held to a draw with just a few minutes remaining. A late corner kick was awarded to Hearts and against the manager's wishes Waugh raced forward in desperation. The ball was hoisted into the box and Waugh leapt like a salmon and connected with the ball on his forehead as sweetly as a nut. The ball flew towards the top corner of the goal and Waugh looked like he was going to be the unlikely hero.

Much to the disbelief and disappointment of the Tynecastle crowd, and Waugh himself, the opposition goalkeeper sprang like a tiger and clutched the net-bound ball just before the net bulged. Realising that Waugh was out of position his opposite number quickly launched the ball forward allowing an opposition striker to latch onto it and walk it into the gaping Hearts net. What a calamity for Waugh! A true 'rebel' indeed.

Believe it or not Auntie Jessie also went through as many of the actions as possible for a 90 year old woman as she recounted that story, and it would mean the world to Jessie if you were able to provide the date and details of that game, while a photograph of Willie Waugh's failed headed attempt on goal would be simply fantastic. Such a photograph would reunite Jessie and Archibald on this earth before the time comes for them to meet once more.

Your assistance is very much appreciated, and we look forward to hearing from you.

Best Wishes,

Struan J. Marjoribanks

HEART OF MIDLOTHIAN PLC
TYNECASTLE STADIUM
GORGIE ROAD
EDINBURGH EH11 2NL
T +44 (0) 870 787 1874
F +44 (0) 131 200 7222
www.heartsfc.co.uk

11 November 2008.

Mr.S.Marjoribanks.

Dear Mr.Marjoribanks,

Thank you for your letter of 3rd.November.

You set us quite a poser this time and although it had a ring of truth we were unable to confirm the story. There are very few of us around who watched Hearts before WW2 and none of the press cuttings we have refer to an incident of that sort.

Unfortunately, I am again, unable to confirm Auntie Jessie's story and at present I cannot get hold of a photograph of Willie Waugh. If you still want a photograph of the goalkeeper in the new year I may have some of our files back in to our store by then, and could check again..

Regards,

Alex.H.Knight.
Club Archivist.

153

19th November 2008

Mr Alex H. Knight
Club Archivist
Heart of Midlothian Football Club
Tynecastle Stadium
McLeod Street
Edinburgh, EH11 2NL

Dear Mr Knight,

Many thanks for your letter dated 11th November 2008. It really is not my intention to monopolise your time, and I'm quite sure that you have a mountain of archives to attend to, so your willingness to help has been tremendously appreciated.

If you could supply a photograph of Willie Waugh in the new year that would be absolutely splendid. Assuming Auntie Jessie is still with us by then I could perhaps have the photograph framed as a 91st birthday present.

Auntie Jessie was slightly disappointed that you were unable to provide the details of that calamitous match in which Waugh's cavalier spirit cost Hearts a point, but sends her thanks for your efforts.

This whole episode involving yourself and Willie Waugh has led to Auntie Jessie casting her mind back to that era rather a lot recently, and she has remembered a little ditty that Archibald would sing regarding Waugh:

Willie Waugh, Willie Waugh,
The best goalkeeper of them aw,
Take a shot, he'll catch the baw,
(She cannot for the life of her remember the final line)

Would you (or any of the older Hearties) happen to know the final line of the song? Poor Auntie Jessie tells me that she has spent the last couple of weeks thinking about practically nothing else, and I am therefore hoping that you will be able to put her out of her misery!

As always we look forward to hearing from you and cannot thank you enough for all of your assistance.

Best Wishes,

Struan J. Marjoribanks

HEART OF MIDLOTHIAN PLC
TYNECASTLE STADIUM
GORGIE ROAD
EDINBURGH EH11 2NL
T +44 (0) 870 787 1874
F +44 (0) 131 200 7222
www.heartsfc.co.uk

16 February 2009.

Mr.S.Marjoribanks,

Dear Mr. Marjoribanks,

Further to my letter of 11 November 2008 I enclose a photocopy of a photograph of Willie Waugh, signed and dated 1938.

He was a solid and reliable goalkeeper, who was signed from Durhamtown Rangers in December 1928. He was loaned to Third Lanark and Hibernian early in his career, but returned to keep Hearts' goal from 1936 to 1941. He was good enough to make a full international appearance against Czechoslovakia in December 1937.

Below is an extract from our 'appearances' files showing his playing career.

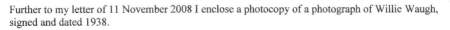

WAUGH William (Willie):-D of B-02/02/1910; Debut-02/01/1933; Service-from Duhamtown Rangers FC 27/12/1928 to Third Lanark FC-loan 09/08/1929 to 29/04/1931 to Third Lanark FC-loan 07/05/1931 to 27/04/1932 to Hibernian FC-loan 28/02/1936 to 27/04/1936-released 14/10/1942.

Season	Scottish Cup	S/outs	League	S/outs	League Cup	S/outs	Europe	S/outs	Total	S/outs	%
1932/1933			2						2		
1933/1934			2	1					2	1	
1936/1937	3	1	36	9					39	10	
1937/1938	1		35	10					36	10	
1938/1939	4		38	8					42	8	
1939/1940			16	3					16	3	
1940/1941			24	3					24	3	
1941/1942			7	2					7	2	
	8	1	160	36					168	37	84.4

I still have not found a source for the last line of the rhyme.

Regards,

Alex.H.Knight.
Club Archivist.

155

22nd February 2009

Mr Alex H. Knight
Club Archivist
Heart of Midlothian Football Club
Tynecastle Stadium
McLeod Street
Edinburgh, EH11 2NL

Dear Mr Knight,

Many, many thanks for your letter dated 16th February 2009 and the photocopy of Willie Waugh's photograph.

Several months had passed but still you remained true to your word. You are a very kind man, and a credit to Heart of Midlothian Football Club. Would Hibernian Football Club's archivist be as professional and considerate is what my family and I are all wondering?

I have now had a chance to show Auntie Jessie your latest letter and the photograph. Admittedly I needed to talk her through Waugh's stats as she couldn't make head nor tail of them (describing them as 'goalkeeping gobbledygook'), but Auntie Jessie's face simply beamed when she saw the photograph.

Indeed, the photograph made such a deep connection with Auntie Jessie that when she saw it she blurted out the full rhyme:

Willie Waugh, Willie Waugh,
The best goalkeeper of them aw,
Take a shot, he'll catch the baw,
Think you can score? Naw, naw

Personally I'm not sure about that last line, but Auntie Jessie seemed quite adamant that it is correct (and I was as rigorous in my cross examination of her as her age would allow). What do you reckon Mr Knight? Is it possible for a ditty from the 1930s to goad the opposition in this way? Football fans of that era usually seem so innocent with their clackers and flat caps, and for that reason I remain sceptical.

We would be delighted to hear your thoughts on this, and many thanks again for everything that you have done for myself and Auntie Jessie.

Best Wishes,

Struan J. Marjoribanks

HEART OF MIDLOTHIAN PLC
TYNECASTLE STADIUM
GORGIE ROAD
EDINBURGH EH11 2NL
T +44 (0) 870 787 1874
F +44 (0) 131 200 7222
www.heartsfc.co.uk

31 March 2009.

Mr.S.Marjoribanks,

Dear Mr Madjoribanks,

Thank you for your recent letter.

Your aunt's little rhyme is almost certainly correct as that was the style in the 1930's. It was the pleasant side of football banter with mixed crowds on terracing. In those days there was not the signing of 'tribal' songs and the first recording of Hearts song was not until 1958.

Thank you for your kind remarks. I don't receive many acknowledgements of letters far less a thank you. Maybe, as I am old enough to have seen Willie Waugh play my approach to enquiries is different.

Regrads,

Alex.H.Knight.
Club Archivst.

157

16 April 2009

16th April 2009

Mr Alex H. Knight
Club Archivist
Heart of Midlothian Football Club
Tynecastle Stadium
McLeod Street
Edinburgh, EH11 2NL

Dear Mr Knight,

Great to hear from you again (your letter dated 31st March 2009) and to read more of your words of wisdom on all things Hearts.

I cannot thank you enough on behalf of Auntie Jessie for verifying the authenticity of her rhyme. She now feels that her last few years/months/weeks/days (delete as applicable) can be enjoyed with the reassurance that she now knows where she is going and who she will meet there.

My other reason for writing was simply to thank you for your thanks. You know, very, very seldom am I thanked for my thanks. So many thanks for that.

I look forward to hearing your thoughts.

Best Wishes,

Struan J. Marjoribanks

END OF CORRESPONDENCE

my **vivid** dream: 25th october 2011

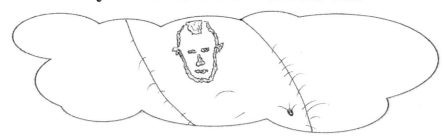

me: it's the strangest thing — i've developed a rash in the shape of
           wayne rooney's head

wife: are you sure it's not ross kemp?

me: no, i'm quite sure it's rooney

me: look doctor, it's definitely wayne rooney. should i be concerned?

doctor: why, do you not like football?

me: well, no, not really

me: hello, yes, i was wondering if you would be interested in a story
           about a rash on my arm that looks like wayne rooney?

journalist: we would only be interested if he is doing something
            inappropriate or vulgar

me: oh bother! this dream just is not going to have a happy ending

Mr Gary Bollan
First Team Manager
Livingston Football Club
Almondvale Stadium
Almondvale Stadium Road
Livingston, EH54 7DN

Dear Mr Bollan

Would you be interested to learn the details if members of your squad had been seen up to what could only be described as 'monkey business' in Edinburgh city centre on a Saturday evening?

Best Wishes,

Struan J. Marjoribanks

Thursday 24th September 2009

LIVINGSTON
FOOTBALL CLUB

ALMONDVALE STADIUM
ALMONDVALE STADIUM ROAD
LIVINGSTON EH54 7D
TELEPHONE: 01506 41700
FACSIMILIE: 01506 41888
www. livingstonfc.co.u

Dear Mr Marjorbanks

I write with regards to your letter dated the 20th September 2009 and would welcome further details from yourself.

I would appreciate if you could call me on the above number.

I look forward to hearing from you.

Yours Faithfully
Livingston Football Club

Gary Bollan
First Team Manager

LIVINGSTON FOOTBALL CLUB
MAIN SPONSOR

LIVINGSTON F.C. LT
ALMONDVALE STADIU
ALMONDVALE STADIUM RO
LIVINGSTON EH54 7
COMPANY REG. NO. 1424

2nd October 2009

Mr Gary Bollan
First Team Manager
Livingston Football Club
Almondvale Stadium
Almondvale Stadium Road
Livingston, EH54 7DN

Dear Mr Bollan

Your letter dated 24th September was most gratefully received. I will be sure to give you a call should I see anything.

Best Wishes,

Struan J. Marjoribanks

162

3rd August 2008

Mr Dave MacKinnon
Chief Executive
Dundee Football Club
Dens Park Stadium
Sandeman Street
Dundee
DD3 7JY

Dear Mr MacKinnon,

Auntie Jessie will be 90 years old on the 11th of September and she is a 'weel kent' (well known) face on the terraces of Dens Park. Many of her children, grandchildren, nieces, nephews, great grandchildren and great nieces and nephews can also be found amongst the Dens Park faithful. I kid you not when I tell you that a truer Dundonian than Auntie Jessie I have yet to meet.

Auntie Jessie lived on the same street as the great Bobby Seith after the war which cemented her love affair with your club. She used to talk about Bobby all the time, but unfortunately her memory is not the same as it used to be. So much so that sadly when asked about her memories of Bobby recently she paused deep in thought and then told a story about a butcher from Broughty Ferry.

I know you value the continued support of your many loyal fans, and as they do not come any more loyal than dear old Auntie Jessie I would like to think that the club would be able to help us celebrate her landmark birthday in a unique and special way. I notice that Dundee play Dunfermline Athletic at Dens Park on the 13th of September and would like to make a simple request regarding this match.

Would it be possible to have t-shirts made up with 'HAPPY 90th BIRTHDAY JESSIE' emblazoned across the chest which could be worn by the first team under their shirts? Then, when Dundee score a goal the team can lift up their famous dark blue shirts revealing their birthday wishes for Auntie Jessie. Can you imagine the joy that this would bring to an old, frail Dundee fan like Auntie Jessie?

I look forward to hearing your thoughts on this idea and hope that you are able to help this birthday dream become a reality. I am very happy to provide the t-shirts if you can get the players on board, and I eagerly await your instructions.

Best Wishes,

Struan J. Marjoribanks

163

DUNDEE FOOTBALL CLUB LTD

Dens Park Stadium Sandeman Street Dundee DD3 7JY Scotland

Football, Telephone: 01382 826104, Admin: 01382 889966, Fax 01382 832284
Marketing & Commercial Department, Telephone: 01382 884450, E-mail dfc@dundeefc.co.uk

Tuesday 19th August 2008

Struan J. Marjoribanks

Dear Mr Marjoribanks,

Great to hear about Auntie Jessie's 90th Birthday and we wish her all the very best.

We would be delighted to help Jessie, by inviting her and a guest to the Dundee FC v Dunfermline Athletic FC game on the 13th September also wishing her best wishes over the Tannoy System and in the Matchday Programme for that game.

Unfortunately, due to League rule on T-Shirts we cannot allow "Happy 90th Birthday Jessie".

Please contact Laura Hayes on 01382 826104 for this to be arranged.

Yours Sincerely
For and on behalf of Dundee Football Club

Dave MacKinnon
Chief Executive

164

Registered in Edinburgh, Scotland No. 4585 VAT Reg. No. 268 3051 56

Ms Laura Hayes
Dundee Football Club
Dens Park Stadium
Sandeman Street
Dundee
DD3 7JY

Dear Ms Hayes,

As you will be aware I received a most touching letter from your leader Mr MacKinnon dated 19th August 2008. The offer to make Auntie Jessie and a friend guests of honour for the match against Dunfermline on 13th September was very kind indeed, and has been greatly appreciated by all of the family.

Unfortunately things have been rather difficult since I wrote to Mr MacKinnon. Auntie Jessie's budgie Arthur passed away quietly on his perch last Sunday, and Jessie has been so upset that she has not spoken since. My brother visited Auntie Jessie yesterday in an attempt to raise her spirits and she refused to speak to him - in fact she threw the television remote control at him and then threw the cup of tea he had made for her against the wall.

Until Auntie Jessie comes out of this deep depression we will be unable to fully assess her state of mind. However, when Buster (her Yorkshire terrier) died in 1987 Auntie Jessie took it so badly that she set her couch on fire and squandered the majority of her life savings on a couple of horse races.

It seems that as one gets older death becomes a bigger and bigger part of one's life, and Auntie Jessie has witnessed so many deaths to those close to her that it now appears to have taken its toll. She has watched on helplessly as friends, family, children, Buster, and now her beloved Arthur have passed away.

I therefore feel that it would be unfair to accept Mr MacKinnon's kind offer as Auntie Jessie just does not seem able, but rest assured Jessie will be made aware of the club's overwhelming generosity when the time is right. If Auntie Jessie were to attend and created a scene within the stadium I would feel terrible – and I would not wish to be responsible for replacing the Dens Park crockery!

Perhaps we could mark Auntie Jessie's 90th birthday in another way, and I therefore wonder if you have ever scattered the ashes of a pet over the Dens Park pitch? We could cremate Arthur (he is in a biscuit tin in Auntie Jessie's flat so this is still possible) and have his ashes scattered over the turf as a mark of respect for Arthur and also to symbolise the circle of life which perhaps Auntie Jessie has now almost also completed.

Please let me know if this might be possible and I will arrange for the cremation and for the ashes to be sent to you at Dens Park.

I look forward to hearing from you, and many thanks again for the club's most generous offer.

Best Wishes,

Struan J. Marjoribanks

165

DUNDEE FOOTBALL CLUB LTD

Dens Park Stadium Sandeman Street Dundee DD3 7JY Scotland

Football, Telephone: 01382 826104, Admin: 01382 889966, Fax 01382 832284
Marketing & Commercial Department, Telephone: 01382 884450, E-mail dfc@dundeefc.co.uk

29th August 2009

Struan J Marjoribanks

███████████
███████████
███████████

Dear Struan,

Thank you for your letter of the 23rd of August.

First of all let me say on behalf of the Club how concerned we are for the health of Auntie Jessie, and we send our best wishes to her in her time of grief.

I have shared your letter with the staff and players at Dundee FC and all are disappointed that they will be unable to meet Auntie Jessie at this time, but look forward to her health being sufficiently improved to make the journey to Dundee in the future.

They have though asked me if you could provide a photograph of Auntie Jessie which we will place in the home dressing room. If you could send an up to date photo it would greatly inspire the team.

With regard to scattering Arthur's ashes at Dens we would be delighted to do so and indeed have involved our Club Chaplain David Scott in the matter to ensure "the circle of life" is closed for Arthur.

I am though concerned that sending Arthur's ashes in the post is not the most reliable and respectful thing to do therefore I have a couple of solutions:

- you or a member of your family can come along to Dens to perform the ceremony
- As I live near you I can collect

If it is the latter I could then possibly meet Auntie Jessie which would be tremendous.

On behalf of the Club I look forward to hearing from you.

Best wishes

David

David Mackinnon
Chief Executive

166

1st September 2008

Mr Dave MacKinnon
Chief Executive
Dundee Football Club
Dens Park Stadium, Sandeman Street
Dundee, DD3 7JY

Dear Mr MacKinnon,

Happy September! I don't know about you but September is my favourite month of the year, and not really for any particular reason - it just is.

I was so thrilled to receive your letter dated 29th August 2009. How time flies as you get older! Knowing that the thoughts of those that matter in Dens Park are with Auntie Jessie is both humbling and touching in equal measure, so many, many thanks.

I dearly wish that I could provide a recent photograph of Auntie Jessie for your dressing room, but this is nigh on impossible I am afraid. Auntie Jessie inexplicably goes to pieces when a camera is produced and weeps uncontrollably for up to three hours thereafter. This has been happening for around fifteen years and had spoiled many Christmas Days until as a family we finally banned cameras in 1999.

Perhaps I could either arrange for a child to draw a picture of Auntie Jessie, or ask Ninewells Hospital to provide a still image of a recent visit from their CCTV camera.

I wholeheartedly agree with you that posting Arthur's ashes would be disrespectful and fraught with postal uncertainty. I do not know what I was thinking about suggesting such a thing, and I am relieved that you had the clarity of mind to prevent certain disaster.

Your offer to meet Auntie Jessie here was also greatly appreciated, but as you will understand she is up yonder. So too was Arthur's rigid little corpse and its whereabouts is now the cause of considerable consternation. Cousin Bryce telephoned Auntie Jessie from Australia in an attempt to arrange the cremation of Arthur. Naturally Auntie Jessie would not speak to Bryce, but her friend Elspeth advised him that Arthur's body went missing last week and that Jessie would only cough when asked where it had gone.

Alas I am in something of a quandary and hope that Chaplain Scott has other duties to perform in the absence of Arthur's ashes. I wonder if perhaps Chaplain Scott could bestride the Dens Park turf and read out this poem which I have penned in Arthur's memory:

> *Budgie baby, wings from heaven,*
> *Budgie child, life unforgiving,*
> *Budgie man, no longer living,*
> *Budgie death, peaceful as snow that's driven*

These may not be words from a holy text, but it was considerably better than Bryce's effort, and perhaps Auntie Jessie will take comfort from them. I look forward as always to hearing your thoughts, and thanks again for all of your generosity.

Best Wishes,

Struan J. Marjoribanks

167

END OF
CORRESPONDENCE

my (house's) appearance on 'through the keyhole'

grossman: (oblivious to weirdness of accent) so let's take a look at
the evidence: the awards, the recipe books, the many priceless objets
d'art, the comedy sign which reads 'don't ask me - i really don't
know', the general opulence. who lives in a house like this? david,
it's over to you.

frosty: (sneering) that house really is magnificent. it is
probably more tastefully decorated than mine, but whose is it?
willie rushton, what do you think?

rushton: gosh, it could only possibly belong to marjoribanks.
struan j. marjoribanks.

studio audience whistle, clap and cheer in the way that only
studio audiences made up predominantly of british pensioners do.

frosty: (impressed) sensational willie!

rushton: (nonchalantly) had to be.

Mr Graham Tatters
Acting Chairman
Elgin City Football Club
Borough Briggs
Elgin, Moray
IV30 1AP

Dear Mr Tatters,

As Acting Chairman I hope that you will be able to assist me with an important request. As you will be aware Elgin City are playing Stenhousemuir at The Briggs (as we call it) on Saturday 18th October.

We have a large family wedding taking place that day in Aberlour, and the groom is not a fan of The City hence the horrific clash of dates. However, my side of the family is literally Elgin City daft, and we have twelve relatives making the journey to the wedding all the way from Canada. There should be another three coming from Australia but my cousin Bryce's family are in a bit of a pickle financially at present, so best not to include them in the potential numbers.

Of the twelve Canadians at least eight of them are fans of Elgin City and they are devastated that after coming all that way they will be in a church while The City take on Stenhousemuir. There are at least fifteen other non-Canadian wedding invitees who would also have otherwise been at The Briggs that day and are equally distraught at the poor planning of the wedding.

Now, Mr Tatters to my request: Would it be at all possible to reschedule the Stenhousemuir match for Sunday 19th October, or better still Wednesday 22nd October (the Canadian contingent are still here then)? I appreciate that this is a big ask but given the notice I would hope that this could be arranged with minimum fuss.

I urge you to think not only of the additional gate money that your club would make if you were able to accommodate us, but also the boost to the local economy that such a large and high-spirited visiting party would generate. Much food and drink would naturally be purchased both in and out of the stadium, not to mention the substantial additional merchandise sales, and knowing my family the local bookmakers would also see an upturn in their takings.

So, Mr Tatters all my hope is in you. If you were able to take this request to your loyal board I would greatly appreciate it and I (along with twelve Canadians and around fifteen non-Canadians) eagerly await your response.

Best Wishes,

Struan J. Marjoribanks

169

ELGIN CITY FOOTBALL CLUB LTD.

BOROUGH BRIGGS - ELGIN - MORAY IV30 1AP TEL : 01343 551114 FAX : 01343 547921

Mr Struan J Marjoribanks

2ND August 2008

Dear Mr Marjoribanks

I thank you for your letter dated 27th July 2008 addressed to Graham Tatters.

I very much appreciate the spirit of the request and the content of your letter. However we do not have the authority to re-arrange a Scottish Football League fixture.

Of course a Referee can postpone a match if he or she determines that the pitch is unsafe and a Club can make representations to the Scottish League in the event of illness to the playing staff but other than that we are duty bound to fulfil the fixture.

On behalf of the Club I hope that you and your family have a super day at the wedding.

If you and any of the Wedding Guests would like to visit the Stadium then please give us a call and we would be delighted to "show you round"

Yours sincerely

Martyn Hunter

Martyn Hunter
Director

REGISTERED OFFICE : BOROUGH BRIGGS ELGIN MORAY IV30 1AP
REGISTERED IN SCOTLAND No. 207126
EMAIL :
elgincityfc@btconnect.com
accountsecfc@btconnect.com

170

7th August 2008

Mr Martyn Hunter
Director
Elgin City Football Club
Borough Briggs
Elgin, Moray
IV30 1AP

Dear Mr Hunter,

Many thanks for your prompt response and your letter dated 2nd August 2008 – if only Elgin City's goalkeeper had such speedy reactions!!!

The kind wishes regarding the wedding day were gratefully received, as was the very kind offer of 'showing us round' The Briggs. These have been relayed to the family and have been greatly appreciated by one and all – Aunt Jessie (nearly 90), for example, was so overwhelmed by your generosity that it reduced her to tears.

Just a word of warning regarding your offer of an impromptu stadium tour: there are some members of the family (such as cousin Bryce) who I would not trust in your inner sanctum due to their light-fingered ways. Do please let me know if any of the family get in touch with you directly so that I can advise you regarding their suitability for the tour.

I respect your decision that it is not the place of the club to re-arrange fixtures, but read with immense interest that the referee and playing staff are able to postpone a game if necessary. I have therefore spoken to Kenny (the most intelligent of the Canadian contingent) and we have come up with the following ideas which could allow the match to be postponed:

1. You contact the Scottish Football League on the Friday advising that nine members of the first team have been struck down with food poisoning after attending the opening of a new Bangladeshi restaurant the night before.

2. We dig a hole in the middle of the pitch on the Friday night (not a huge hole - perhaps five feet in diameter). The referee would inspect the pitch on the Saturday and deem the pitch to be dangerous. We would then repair the pitch immediately - three of the Canadians are landscape gardeners so this would be very easy.

3. You announce on the Friday that four members of the Elgin City 'extended family' (best to keep it vague) have been lost at sea during a round-the-world boat race, and that it would not be right to play a football match under these circumstances. Then announce on the Saturday night (after the game has been postponed) that they have been found safe and well allowing the resumption of football matches.

So what do you think Mr Hunter – are we on? As you can see the Marjoribanks clan are a resourceful lot if nothing else. These plans appear to be foolproof so I very much look forward to hearing your thoughts and (hopefully) giving the family the good news.

Best Wishes,

Struan J. Marjoribanks

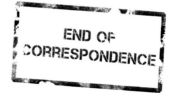

END OF
CORRESPONDENCE

171

Pastor Michael Rollo
Club Chaplain
Stenhousemuir Football Club
Ochilview Park
Gladstone Road
Stenhousemuir
Falkirk, FK5 4QL

Dear Pastor Rollo,

It is with considerable sorrow that I inform you that Cousin Bryce is going through an extremely difficult and protracted court case in Australia.

I shall not burden you with the ins and outs of the trial, but I am writing to you as I feel that as a man of God you will uphold the most Christian of values: *'judge not lest ye be judged.'*

Stenhousemuir FC is Bryce's true love, and the club remains very dear to his heart despite many years of skirting with the law *Down Under*. This court case is Bryce's most gruelling one yet, and such has been its weight upon his once broad shoulders that I now declare Cousin Bryce a broken man.

As Club Chaplain of Stenhousemuir FC would you be able to offer a few words to Bryce which may bring him hope and strength at this impossibly difficult time? Bryce says he didn't do it and although history may not be on his side we believe him.

Any message would be very gratefully received and I can forward it on when I next send him his favourite crisps and the Stenhousemuir FC newspaper clippings which I have saved for him.

I look forward to hearing from you and I thank you in advance for finding it in your heart to offer warmth and humanity where so many others (most notably Julia) have shamefully turned their backs.

Best Wishes,

Struan J. Marjoribanks

LARBERT PENTECOSTAL CHURCH A.O.G
In Fellowship with Assemblies of God (GB)
A registered Scottish Charity No SCO 28111

www.aoglarben.org
Tel:- 01324 563367

Mr Struan J Marjoribanks

███████████

███████████

20th October 2009

Dear Struan

Thank you for your letter of 11th October re Cousin Bryce. I appreciate you taking the time to write, and I apologise for the late reply as I have been on holiday. It is difficult to know where to begin and what really to say, in response to your question. I feel a bit like a doctor being asked to give a prescription for a patient I have never met or consulted. I will however do my best.

First of all I have begun to pray for Bryce, that God will help him. One of the simplest and most helpful of phrases is that "God is only a prayer away". In the Bible God tells us to "call upon me in the day of trouble" and in Psalm 46 we are reminded that "God is our refuge and strength and an ever present help in time of trouble". In his epistle, James writes that if we draw near to God, He will draw near to us.

I know all these scriptures to be true, from personal experience. I know that God does want to help His people. Over the summer months we have been watching a series of DVD's on prayer from Brooklyn Tabernacle in New York. They contain some absolutely amazing testimonies of people who have been set free from all kinds of situations.

There are some great books out there. Nick Gumbel (Alpha) for example has written a book on Searching Issues. Phil Yancey wrote a book called "where is God when it hurts?". A good book can be a good friend when times are tough. The Bible itself in a contemporary translation is unsurpassed. I enclose a leaflet entitled "where to look in the Gospels" which points to words of comfort in troubled times. I also enclose a copy of the devotional book "word for Today" which has a simple reading for every day of the month for three months. This can be ordered direct or viewed online.

I would say Bryce's biggest comfort at the moment is to know that people like yourself believe him, believe in him, and care for him. That's wonderful. I hope that the enclosed literature and the few lines above will be helpful. My contact details are at the foot of this letter if you require any further assistance.

Yours Sincerely

MICHAEL G. ROLLO
Senior Minister.

Pastoral Team
Michael G. Rollo (Senior Pastor) A.C.I.B.S.; Dip Theo. C.D.R.S. "Beracah", 12 Carrick Place, Carron, Falkirk. FK2 8HT. Tel - 01324-885934
Diane Rollo "Beracah" 12 Carrick Place, Carron Falkirk. FK2 8HT. Tel:- 01324-885934
John Daniel (Assistant Pastor) BA (Hons), 79 Burnhead Road, Larbert FK5 4BD. Tel:- 01324-551012
John Rollo (Youth Pastor) Bsc (Hons), 11, Ardvreck Place, Carron FK2 8BS. Tel:- 01324-870868

'At last...
the
WORD
for today
*to be broadcast to the entire
nation on UCB DAB Digital Radio'*

Bob Gass

Where to look
in the Gospels

NOV

SCOISH
BIBLE SOCIETY
The Word for the world

Pastor Michael Rollo
Senior Minister
12 Carrick Place
Carron
Falkirk, FK2 8BT

Dear Pastor Rollo,

Your letter of 20th October brought such an invigorating and renewed sense of hope to our family that my wife literally wept with joy. Being a man I felt that I should not cry, but I don't mind telling you that my eyes required dabbing with a handkerchief once or twice when nobody was looking.

I telephoned Cousin Bryce the day your letter arrived and he too was bowled over. Bryce telephoned me yesterday with a lovely story which I'd like to share with you. Bryce had quoted your letter to his youngest daughter Fontonella, advising her that 'if we draw near to God, He will draw near to us.' Upon hearing this Fontonella opened up her sketch pad, laid some crayons on it and then sat perfectly still staring at the blank pages. When Bryce asked Fontonella what she was doing she replied without a second's hesitation: 'waiting for God to start drawing of course.' Isn't that just adorable?

Thanks so much for the advice given to Bryce about books he could take comfort from. Obviously he has read the Bible and it is a good one, but he hasn't read the Nick Gumbel book yet and says that he'll probably ask for that one for Christmas. Bryce has read the Phil Yancey book and although he felt that it 'lacked pace in the middle' and was 'guilty of moments of self-indulgent grandiosity' that over all it was a worthwhile read. Bryce gave the Yancey book 7 out of 10 incidentally (Bryce always rates books, meals, women's figures etc in this manner).

I must also thank you for enclosing the useful and charming booklets 'Where To Look In The Gospels' and 'Word For Today'. I'm due to send Bryce his Monster Munch and Stenhousemuir FC newspaper cuttings next week so I will be sure to enclose the booklets.

Cousin Bryce had one question for you, and I hope that you don't mind me asking you it on his behalf. *As Club Chaplain of Stenhousemuir FC do you pray for the club's good fortune on the pitch, and if so how do you interpret those prayers being seldom answered?* I personally felt that his question was a smidgen cheeky given all that you have done for him, but due to the impossibly stressful predicament in which Bryce finds himself I promised to ask you.

In a time when we oft feel let down by the human race you have taken the time to extend a hand of friendship to a family on its knees, and I cannot thank you enough for that. I hope to hear from you soon, but should you feel that you have already done enough I will understand.

Best Wishes,

Struan J. Marjoribanks

LARBERT PENTECOSTAL CHURCH A.O.G

In Fellowship with Assemblies of God (GB)
A registered Scottish Charity No SCO 28111

www.aoglarbert.org
Tel:- 01324 563367

Mr Struan J Marjoribanks

███████████
███████████
███████████

29th October 2009

Dear Struan

Thank you very much for your very welcome letter. I was pleased it was a blessing and was touched by your kind comments. It also brought a smile to my face on a number of occasions while reading it through.

In reply to Bryce's question re my prayers for SFC, and the apparent lack of a positive answer from the Lord. I have to confess that I do not really pray for results on the pitch. Maybe that's why they are not doing so well and I need to start!

I believe my responsibilities are to be there to serve the Lord primarily, through the Club's invitation, and to provide spiritual help if or when required. So I try to make myself available. I have had a pretty hectic schedule of late, but try to go to the home games, and show up in the background at training. I want to be visible without being a nuisance. I am also conscious that chaplains from opposing teams could also be praying for their teams to win. Although I enjoy football, there are more important things in life, even though some in Scotland, and around the world, think football is the be all and end all. I am there for the times when people struggle with all kinds of difficulties, and hopefully can help.

Bryce's question is a valid question and I can assure you I have seen many answers to prayer, and there have been times when God has not answered in the manner I would have preferred, but has answered nevertheless. I have also seen some pretty spectacular answers to prayer.

Please give my regards to your wife and to your cousin and His family. His daughter's response reminded me of the man who prayed "lead us not into Thames Station" instead of "temptation" in the Lord's prayer. Tell Bryce, that failure isn't when we fail, but when we don't get back up after failure. *"Micah 7:8 Do not gloat over me, my enemy! Though I have fallen, I will rise . Though I sit in darkness, the LORD will be my light.*

Yours Sincerely

MICHAEL G. ROLLO
Senior Minister

176

Pastoral Team
Michael G. Rollo (Senior Pastor) A.C.I.B.S., Dip Theo. C.D.R.S. "Beracah", 12 Carrick Place, Carron Falkirk. FK2 8BT. Tel:- 01324-885934
Diane R. Rollo "Beracah" 12 Carrick Place, Carron, Falkirk. FK2 8BT. Tel:- 01324-885934
John Daniel (Assistant Pastor) BA (Hons), 79 Burnhead Road, Larbert. FK5 3BD. Tel:- 01324-551012
John Rollo (Youth Pastor) Bsc (Hons), 11 Ardvreck Place, Carron FK2 8BS. Tel:- 01324-870868

Faith Like Potatoes The Story of Angus Buchan - £14.67

Frank Rautenbach leads a strong cast as Angus Buchan, a Zambian farmer of Scottish heritage who leaves his farm in the midst of political unrest and racially-charged land reclaims and travels south with his family to start a better life in KwaZulu Natal, South Africa. With nothing more than a caravan on a patch of land, and help from his foreman, Simeon Bhengu, the Buchan family struggle to settle in a new country. Faced with ever-mounting challenges, hardships and personal turmoil, Angus quickly spirals down into a life consumed by anger, fear and destruction. Based on the inspiring true story by Angus Buchan, the book was adapted for the big screen by Regardt van den Bergh and weaves together the moving life journey of a man who, like his potatoes, grows his faith, unseen until the harvest. Angus Buchan wrote and published the book *Faith Like Potatoes* in 1998. It continues to touch people from all age groups, social groups, backgrounds and cultures as is evident by its continued sales and the number of emails, faxes and letters that Angus receives from readers on a daily basis. This powerful DVD includes a gripping 54 minute documentary on the real life Angus Buchan, the making of Faith Like Potatoes, director and cast commentary, deleted scenes and more.

Fireproof Your Life - £14.67

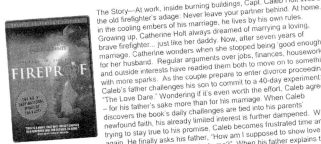

Fireproof is an action-packed love story about a firefighter, his wife... and a marriage worth rescuing! In US cinemas it touched the hearts - and souls - of millions of filmgoers.

The Story—At work, inside burning buildings, Capt. Caleb Holt lives by the old firefighter's adage: Never leave your partner behind. At home, in the cooling embers of his marriage, he lives by his own rules. Growing up, Catherine Holt always dreamed of marrying a loving, brave firefighter... just like her daddy. Now, after seven years of marriage. Catherine wonders when she stopped being 'good enough' for her husband. Regular arguments over jobs, finances, housework, and outside interests have readied them both to move on to something with more sparks. As the couple prepare to enter divorce proceedings, Caleb's father challenges his son to commit to a 40-day experiment: "The Love Dare." Wondering if it's even worth the effort, Caleb agrees – for his father's sake more than for his marriage. When Caleb discovers the book's daily challenges are tied into his parents' newfound faith, his already limited interest is further dampened. While trying to stay true to his promise, Caleb becomes frustrated time and again. He finally asks his father, "How am I supposed to show love to somebody who constantly rejects me?" When his father explains that this is the love Christ shows to us, Caleb makes a life-changing commitment to love God. And with God's help he begins to understand what it means to truly love his wife. But is it too late to fireproof his marriage? His job is to rescue others. Now Caleb Holt is ready to face his toughest job ever...rescuing his wife's heart.

177

Pastor Michael Rollo
Senior Minister
12 Carrick Place
Carron
Falkirk, FK2 8BT

Dear Pastor Rollo,

I cannot thank you enough for taking the time to get back in touch, and your letter of 29th October was received as warmly as ever.

I was tickled pink that you took pleasure from my last letter, and I could not agree more that the Lord is our light. Thank goodness He doesn't turn the clocks back and give us an hour's less love and direction just because it is winter! 'Good old God' I say.

I was fascinated to read about your duties at Stenhousemuir FC and of your awareness of other club chaplains all vying for the Lord to 'stick one in the back of the pokey' (as my dear old Papa would have put it) for their own team. Perhaps the hugely successful football clubs such as Manchester United, Real Madrid and Steaua Bucharest have a history of ruthless and single-minded club chaplains who have made it their business to ensure that the Lord has little time to answer the prayers of the poor and needy clubs.

Your 'Thames Station' gag had us Marjoribanks' guffawing into our Shreddies I can tell you. However, when I told it to Cousin Bryce the old sourpuss just groaned and said that he had a better religious joke. I didn't actually get Bryce's joke. He said that there were two nuns cycling down a cobbled street. The first nun says 'I've never come this way before.' The second nun replies 'must be the cobbles.'

I will not take up any more of your valuable time, but I must thank you from the bottom of my heart for offering support and hope to Cousin Bryce and both of our families at this difficult time. Your own family is lucky to have such a kind and warm man at its helm.

May God be with you, and if I suddenly notice Stenhousemuir FC racing up through the divisions and playing in the Champions League I'll know that you decided to have a word in His shell-like.

Best Wishes,

[signature]

Struan J. Marjoribanks

END OF CORRESPONDENCE